WHAT'S INSIDE MATTERS

HAZEL ROBERTS

Contents

Introduction

Have you ever felt insecure about yourself or the society you live in today?

This book highlights just how precious and important we all are as individuals, demonstrating in simple terms why we need to consider the inside of a person, rather than automatically judging them by their physical appearance.

My mission is to help other people. Being able to write about specific subjects that are close to my heart is a privilege and lifetime goal of mine. I am passionate about trying to make the world a better place.

Within the following chapters, you can expect to find lots of useful information about self-help, mindfulness, well-being, personal growth, family values, society in general, mental health, body positivity, happiness and confidence.

My book is primarily aimed at women, but I genuinely hope that males of any age will find it helpful, interesting and informative.

The fact that I'm just a regular, everyday person with no

celebrity status will, I hope, help you trust me. I'm not trying to sell you anything, least of all myself. I was born and grew up in Manchester and lived there until I was 31. I am now aged 55 and live in North Wales with my family.

I am a mother, wife, step-mum, daughter, sister, auntie, step-grandma, parent to my parents (both aged 91) and, last but by no means least, a business woman. During my lifetime I have interacted with thousands of people *and I mean thousands,* mainly through working and travelling.

Compiling this book, which is ultimately aimed at informing and helping other people, has actually *and unintentionally* helped me on a personal level, too. It has fundamentally changed my life. During the process I was able to face up to my very own deep-rooted 'inner demons' and acknowledge the fact that they do actually exist. In a funny way, this has been part of my healing process, allowing me to 'let go'.

Throughout my writing journey the world has definitely changed, and I have regularly questioned where we are all heading. I've deeply pondered whether I, or indeed anyone, can make a real difference to society. As well as thinking about the world, I have wondered what made me think and feel the way that I do now.

I am not afraid to speak out, but I would *never*, ever choose to offend or hurt anybody. I am simply expressing my own opinions, and freedom of speech is very important for us all.

No two people view the world in precisely the same way; even people from within the same family have a slightly different opinion or 'take on life'. Just being you does make a difference in this world, and to that end, no one can replicate you; nor can they do exactly what you do.

At a glance, human beings appear to look similar to one another; however, as individuals we are entirely different – all with unique souls. Within each of us is a distinct concoction of coded information, biochemicals, specific genes, DNA, personality traits, thoughts, feelings and emotions.

It is obvious that the world's population has deeply held differences, and that may never change. People are born into such very varied circumstances, but despite this we can still have mutual respect and understanding towards one another. We all have a place in this life, along with every single blade of grass, grain of sand, pebble on the beach, and every plant, animal and tree.

Although I now understand just how precious we all are, during my lifetime I have faced many personal struggles, including whether I do 'fit in'. I am now at the stage where I feel prepared to share some of them with you, in the hope that many of the things I've learned may be useful to you.

I will talk you through a few of my own observations and prove to you that it is possible to get through real personal challenges, showing you how I have ended up in a much better place.

Whilst writing this book, (which has taken me several years), I have struggled with anxiety and self-doubt. I admit that for most of the time I have had a fuzzy head. I am not sure whether that is down to the fact that I have so much stress in my life – juggling work and family, being a part time carer for my elderly parents, running a business, the menopause, being a mother and a step-mum – or to memory loss due to my hormones or drinking so much red wine (or all of the above mixed together).

In the past I have drunk wine as a coping mechanism, simply in order to escape, relax, switch off and forget about my daily struggles. Putting my own advice into action has reduced my wine intake, thankfully.

It has been so hard to set time aside, to stop, sit down and put pen to paper amongst so much going on! At times I have felt like running away, but instead I have wrestled with my emotions and innermost thoughts, locked myself away in a quiet place in order to write, or even driven to the top of a nearby mountain to get some peace and quiet. I have gathered together all my observations and scribbled down my theories.

Nowadays my memory is failing me *it's a bit like a sieve*, and because I have been constantly tired, it has not been easy to retain information. Sometimes just constructing chapters was challenging.

Thoughts constantly popped up in the back of my mind, and I was conscious of the fact that I ought to be doing many other things instead. I constantly felt guilty, but *I just needed to write*. Something deep down kept telling me to carry on. It is so important to listen to that voice inside your head, that gut instinct, which is a crucial, priceless and magical thing. If we choose to completely ignore it, we may seriously limit achieving our goals.

People don't have time to listen, so as a consequence of this

I long to share some of my wisdom within the pages of this book. I hope to make some improvements to other people's lives. I write based on who I am and what I have learnt, it's a piece of work that represents me.

Luckily, my inner motivation, self-belief and drive have enabled me to keep going. Yes, they have all taken a beating along the way, but they have come out the other side. *You* can do this too.

Whilst reading this book you will discover a powerful message throughout: what is inside your heart and head really does matter, and we'll discover why.

Grasping what is important in life is a gift, a key factor in finding happiness. It also enables you to understand more about who you really are and what you might want from life.

Society appears to be gripped by materialism and does not really care enough about what is real anymore. Social media in particular, and the sheer **power** it has over us, is a good example. Although it has many good points and I use it every day, sometimes it can be difficult to know the difference between someone real and someone fake.

People tend to hide behind a fake profile, possibly too scared to reveal their true colours. This may be out of fear of rejection, or maybe they are petrified of being judged. I find this awfully sad and distressing.

I hope to strengthen and develop your perception of your own self-worth. I don't want you to suffer feeling uncomfortable, confused or brainwashed, and not knowing who to believe in or trust.

When people compare themselves to others (especially on social media), they may feel envy or jealousy. These negative thoughts are unhealthy, crushing any possibility of being happy, content and living a carefree life.

Pressure surrounds us every day, to look and behave a certain way. If we learnt how to accept ourselves and value our own existence, then maybe we wouldn't need to always be comparing and competing with one another.

The insatiable desire to keep up with having this and doing that, this consumer culture, fuelled by the media, is slowly crushing us. It is critical that we understand how and why we are being misguided and corrupted in such a devious way. I truly believe that the way in which we have been conditioned is extremely damaging and unnecessary, and that it's now time for change.

The media bullies want us to worry about how we look, our weight, skin, hair and teeth; they are exploiting our weaknesses. In order to feel accepted, we are encouraged to spend more money. People worry about whether they have the latest thing, and there is so much emphasis on the outside of a person, including things like clothes, shoes, handbags, make-up, jewellery, nails, eyelashes, breast size and eyebrows.

We need to stand up to this brainwashing. Being force fed a set of ideals is not the answer to happiness.

For most of us, just getting by from day to day is hard enough anyway, don't you think? Each day can be a continuous seesaw of events, with things thrown at us when we are least expecting them. The ups and downs can be quite enough to contend with, so why do we choose to make it even more complicated? Maybe we need to stop and take a moment to think it through and find the right balance.

It's important to avoid falling into the trap of comparing who you are and where you are from. What will that achieve, anyway? Surely more self-doubt and unhappiness, which could develop into all kinds of health complications, physical and mental.

Mental health is already a significant social problem, which sadly only a small percentage of society is acknowledging, never mind addressing. It is a serious problem which is rapidly growing, and we only seem to hear about the tip of the iceberg.

It's vital to hang on to your originality – who you were born to be. We need to look at solutions like self-love and self-respect. Longing to be someone else is a complete waste of who *you* are. Try to be recognised for who you are, what you are inside as a person, not just the way you look. Precious time and energy can be wasted watching others.

It is extremely tempting (I know) to go along with this fairy-tale illusion. Many individuals look as though they are in a trance, aimlessly following the crowd, preoccupied with the lives of celebrities, rather than their own.

This exhausting pace, together with hypnosis by the mass media, is hard to keep up with, and sometimes, instead of facing up to our own reality and planning for the future, we get distracted and side-tracked.

I hope to show you ways to conserve your good energy and use it wisely to guide you towards your own path, not to follow the route of others.

I want to dedicate what's left of my own life, to helping you become more aware of the pitfalls and the candy-coated lifestyle many aspire to be part of. The truth is, it's not real at all; in my opinion it's just make-believe.

It can be a lonely, sometimes unpleasant journey, going against the majority, but believe me, it will be worth it in the end. I'm not going to lie; in the past I have struggled with all this pressure too, but now I look back and laugh at how silly and insignificant it feels. Level-headed individuals like me, who have learnt the hard way from their mistakes, need to stick together, guarding and protecting the next generation!

If we are saying *no* to the use of plastic within our environment, then maybe we should be saying no to plastic people too, if you catch my drift.

We can't completely change the world, but we can all try to make more sense of it, and perhaps improve it. By going back to basics, appreciating what's inside your heart and your head, and focusing on what is inside a human being, life could have more value.

Day after day, people are suffering from negative thoughts about their physical appearance, which can wear them down. Emotional stability and self-esteem are so fragile. In Chapter Two of the book I will give you an example of this, which will involve using a blindfold.

Seeking inner happiness, strength and confidence really is the way forward; it can and will improve your life. I understand that it's not that simple; there really is no magic wand. But I know it's possible – that there is a logical way to begin a new approach. Happy mind = happier life.

Within the book I share some of my weaknesses and admit to my vulnerabilities. In doing so, I hope to encourage you to avoid similar situations.

As humans, we tend to be constantly over-critical of ourselves. This needs to stop, as it can make us ill. Hang-ups and self-doubt can cripple positivity and creativity. This constant battle inside our heads eats away at us like a vicious cancer.

It looks quite serious from where I am standing, and unless we get involved and help, at least in some small way, we could be on the brink of an epidemic of self-hate, anxiety and depression. Sadly, this is reflected in the number of horror stories we hear of eating disorders, self-harming and, in many cases, suicides.

I feel **very** strongly about these social problems that belong to us all, and can totally identify with vulnerable, desperate individuals. For most of my adult life I have judged myself, fretting and suffering, having experienced years and years of self-doubt and low self-esteem. I have upset myself so much with worry, and wasted precious time and energy focusing on nonsensical, negative, irrelevant dilemmas, whispering uncontrollably within my subconscious mind.

I have dwelled on things like 'Do I fit in? Is my body good enough? Am I too tall or too fat? I have no waist, I'm not girly or petite enough. I look like a man, are my feet too big? Why am I stones heavier than perhaps my body was designed to be?' It just goes on…

Feeling negative about my body image is bad news. My thoughts have unfortunately been preoccupied with images which exaggerate my physical defects. When other people look at me, I might look confident and positive on the outside, but on the inside, it has not always been the case. Nowadays I worry less about what other people think of me, which is empowering. I now need to empower others to feel good about themselves and demonstrate ways to avoid influences that are toxic to their self-esteem. Read on to discover how *you* can do this, too.

Once you have recognised that there needs to be a change, things will become clearer. It's an exciting prospect and a wonderful opportunity to say goodbye to deep-rooted insecurities. Remember, you *do* have a choice.

Imagine you are at a crossroads in life.

Option **1**: Turn right.

You can head towards a positive way of thinking about who you are: happy with your choice, optimistic, upbeat, content and in tune with self-awareness, clearly appreciative of what you already have.

Or

Option **2**: Turn left.

You can choose the unhappy route: a hopeless, much tougher journey, constantly questioning who you are, feeling angry, jealous, bitter, hard done by and disillusioned, focused on someone else's life and not your own.

Why choose Option **2**? Try to avoid criticising yourself and hating who you are.

Focus more on Option **1** *or at least be aware of each direction*.

Take the first step

I am thrilled and enthusiastic for you; good energy is contagious. The power is already in your hands, heart and head – you just couldn't see or believe it before.

Take it from me: contentment and inner peace can be a state of mind. By simply changing the way you think and behave, you could become a happier person.

You *can* do this. I will prove to you that it's okay to be just as you are.

Why not use my strength and determination to guide you through these rough times? It will allow you to enhance and improve your happiness levels, and then pass that positive energy on to others. It makes complete sense to invest in your own mind and body, rather than dreaming and wishing for someone else's life. Time is precious and so are *you*.

Chapter One

Being You in a Fake World

From time to time, you might be tempted to ask yourself, 'Do I honestly fit in? Is there room for me in this world?' I have done it myself, many times. Let me stop you there.

Well, of course you fit in and of course there is room for you, and for that matter, what's inside your head and your heart means so much more than you may think it does.

I need to grab your attention and explain just how precious and important *you* are. A lot of this boils down to you having self-belief and confidence. These are not easy things to measure, and they vary a lot from person to person. It is not a straightforward thing to teach, either – for example, it depends on how much self-confidence you have already.

Once you have analysed the amount you think you have, I can demonstrate new ways in which to grow it. A huge part of being happy, confident and content is loving and accepting who *you* are.

As I have aged, it has become clear to me just how vulnerable and fragile the individuals within our society are becoming. Things are constantly changing, and they are so uncertain, I wonder at times which way we are heading. I don't think anybody really knows.

As the world continues to waver, becoming more unstable and fake, I believe that it is vital for us as human beings to feel enlightened and grounded; we need a sense of belonging, reality, purpose and awareness. The world's population has deeply held differences, but we can still have mutual respect and empathy for one another.

If we want our communities to be better places to live in for our families and children, then we need to take some action ourselves. We shouldn't be relying on society to do it.

Courageous individuals, everyday people like you and me, *can* make a difference, and words of encouragement can change the future by causing a ripple effect, a bit like throwing a stone into a still millpond. It is important to be conscious of how other people, including our leaders, dictate and control our lives, and it's essential that we are aware of the sheer power they have, (not necessarily the best power.)

Before we discuss this further, maybe just stop for a few seconds, take a deep breath and clear your mind. I will then lift the lid on what I believe to be society's mass cover-up. This may be a shock, but at least that way we can take a quick glimpse underneath the sugar candy coating that our phoney world of commercialisation, advertising and media has created.

It's like a mask, made from papier mâché, with layer after

layer of fabrication, distorting and carefully covering up what is actually going on in the lives of *real* people.

What a revelation… and as we investigate a little further, peeling away a few more layers, the barefaced truth and the magnitude of this brilliant disguise is exposed.

It's tempting to slam the lid straight back down, leaving the problem for another time, or for someone else to solve – but who is that someone?

I am asking you, as well as asking myself, shouldn't we all be getting involved in helping to put right this global mess? Are we in denial? It's not healthy to carry on living like this, is it?

Do we push the lid back down, cover everything up again, add a bit of glitter and some sparkles, then leave it all for another generation? Or do we tackle it head-on? This is just one of the home truths which I think the public needs to face up to, in today's crazy, fake world.

I am not writing this to upset you or to sound depressing and negative. I simply want to highlight awareness of what is happening, right under our noses. We are somehow too busy to even notice.

In my opinion, some of these problems stem from how we have been raised from childhood, dreaming our lives away and being continuously exploited by advertising and the media. If we found out at an earlier age that life is not a box of chocolates or a sweet bed of roses (some *do* find that out, of course), our later lives might not be such a shock and disappointment. It's okay to have dreams; they are an important part of mapping out and planning our future. However, many other things are equally important; it's not just about how we look and what we own. If only our eyes saw souls, instead of 'bodies', how different the world would be.

It would be beneficial to teach younger children things like self-belief and awareness, positive attitude, tolerance and well-being. All these things are very important for survival, as well as how to live alongside other human beings with empathy and dignity.

The harsh reality is that kids need to know how to be tougher, and to learn much better coping mechanisms. Money and health should be addressed too, as well as how to deal with challenges, obstacles and difficulties. Let's not pretend that there will be no hardships. (I do acknowledge that some people are doing these things already.)

If young people are dreaming their days away, or perhaps thinking that the world owes them a living, then they won't get very far. Some kids are not as fortunate as others, and don't always get the support they need at a young age; they may be born into a difficult situation.

All the more reason to find something or someone to believe in, remembering to start with yourself. Grasping the value of self-worth is crucial. When you have it and feel strong and prepared inside, nobody can make you feel meaningless. This will be your comfort blanket through life (we all need one of those). When you feel proud of yourself, safe in the knowledge that you have a sense of responsibility and integrity, you will feel happier and more secure.

There is far too much sadness in the world right now. In

many ways we have become too materialistic, yet for many reasons we often think we don't have enough.

Mindset is also extremely powerful, sometimes getting overlooked. A person's general outlook on life has a significant effect on their ability to succeed or fail. Thoughts control our feelings, and subsequently feelings and emotions control our behaviour. Emotions and attitude can have a direct effect on how reality unfolds.

Instead of focusing on reality, we tend to dwell on insignificant things such as vanity and body image. These subjects can take complete control of our thought processes. Why do we obsess over other people's appearance, body shape or size? Surely, comparing ourselves to others is damaging and unhealthy?

Physical appearance is far too high up the list, in my opinion. It undoubtedly dominates our first take on others. When we meet another human being, we automatically scan our eyes up and down their body and face, our brains programmed to judge within an instant. Why can't we stop this robotic mind-set, think again and see a little further than the outer packaging? We constantly and obsessively analyse each other. How rude, shallow and sad. It would be much kinder to care about the inside of that human. The population continues with this vanity fiasco. Many are terrified of being labelled as boring or plain, going to great lengths to achieve the perfect image.

There is so much needless damage being done. It is a perfect example of mass corruption at its worst – completely false on so many levels. There is so much more to life other than just appearance. This will become clearer as the book goes on.

Impressionable minds are being manipulated (starting from a very early age) and slowly becoming polluted by advertising, imagery and peer pressure.

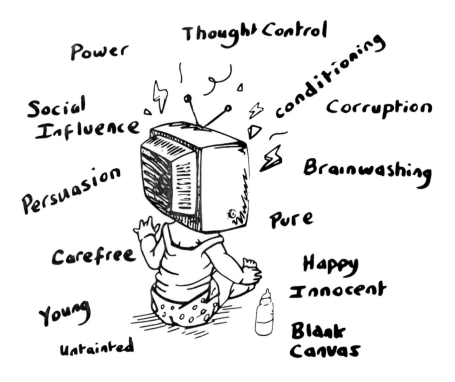

Every single day, our young people are being influenced, without us realising. Unfortunately, we are under a spell, a manufactured illusion.

This problem was gradually beginning to raise its ugly head when I was a teenager, but now it has sadly reached epidemic proportions. Social media is having a catastrophic effect on young people's mental health and well-being. I am convinced that the vast majority of people are not at all happy with the way things are heading. Some people are at breaking point with it all, but still, nobody seems willing to challenge the system.

Children need to know the difference between what's real and what's fake. Many parts of the world are obsessed with body image and, in particular, cosmetic surgery.

To be brutally honest, in many cases it is a complete waste of time, money and energy.

It's safe to say that 'body image' and first impressions dominate our thought processes every single minute of every day. I guess you knew that already.

You are judged on what you are wearing. Is your hair acceptable, are your teeth white enough, have you got a slim waist, do you fit in, do you have lots of friends or followers on social media, or, to be quite frank, how does your bottom measure up? For goodness' sake, can someone tell me what's going on here – why are we still putting up with all this s...?

Does it matter if you are rear of the year? Does it matter if you don't have gigantic breasts? What if you don't fit into any of these categories? What if you already struggle with an inferiority complex? Why should you be made to feel inadequate? We all know that this goes on, but why is it honestly that important?

Does anybody actually care or spare a thought about just how insecure individuals are feeling right now? I mean really vulnerable, unhappy and broken... It's no wonder many are

d mentally scarred and damaged. It's easy to see
'e and sensitive people turn to self-harming,
⌣ of prescription drugs (are we a nation on anti-depressant pills?) or simply drinking alcohol to relax (like me) or forget, or alternatively to excessive eating for comfort or undereating as a form of coping. Many individuals are depressed and have become reliant on, and in some cases addicted to, drugs, in order to make it through each day, as a way of escaping from or coping with reality.

Why have we made this reality? Why have we manufactured such a fake existence?

I believe that we need to be so much more supportive and understanding of these issues. Mental health, as well as physical, should be discussed far more openly. We have a costly epidemic on our hands which is not going to go away anytime soon. It will spiral even further out of control, unless we do something about it *now*. We read facts and figures, but nobody really knows what the reality is.

Please don't turn a blind eye to humanity's cry. We are all in this together, and we all need to take ownership of the problem. I'm not too scared to tackle this, are you? I have a strong desire to help my fellow citizens.

The child of today is the adult of tomorrow.

Luckily there are changes that we can make, even if we start with small ones in our own circles and communities. There really is hope. Alone, we can do so little; but together we can achieve so much more. I hope that by reading this, we will have more awareness. The fundamental question is, do we really want change? How much do we want it?

Take some time out to think about this and discuss it with family and friends. Throughout the book, I will be challenging your thoughts on the subject.

It sounds ridiculous, I know, but a particularly tough challenge that we are up against in today's world is being able to be ourselves in an environment that is constantly trying to make us into somebody else. We are not just 'our bodies' – we are more than that. Standing up for yourself, being brave, accepting what you look like and realistically having the courage to carry it off, is achievable.

The diet industry is responsible for grooming and shaping our society, and as a result of this we are all suffering and paying the price. Damage has been done already, but it's never too late. We can take control and speak out. That's exactly what I am doing right now.

These multi-billion-pound industries need to recognise that beauty does not have a size or a weight limit; it does not have a rule book; there really is no right or wrong.

Body image can be whatever we want it to be. Let's celebrate body diversity: size, shape, age, race, gender and so on. Why should we be controlled by these manipulative giants, sucking on our guilt?

Some poor souls can spend their entire lives feeling guilty, hungry, angry, fat, skinny, even worrying themselves to death in some extreme cases. As I asked earlier, *why* are we focusing on these trivial topics, when there is *so* much more meaning to life?

We all have our worst bits and best bits – that is what makes us who we are – simple humans with real bodies, hearts and minds, flesh and blood, skin and bone.

We tend to be so critical of our unique naked flesh, delivered as we were into the world from our mothers' wombs. Stand proud and grateful for what you have been born with. I am sure that our mothers, whether alive or dead, would be hurt and disappointed if they knew that we were trying so desperately to change things.

What's wrong with marks, spots, dimples and blemishes? The odd scar here and there is evidence of things that have happened to us along the way. Stretch marks and cellulite are perfectly normal and natural. A cuddly tummy, a chunky waist, a long or crooked nose, wonky teeth, big ears, a limp, who cares?

Don't be ashamed; don't hide yourself. Remember: nothing in life is perfect. Fruits are all different shapes and sizes, aren't they? Some look good on the outside but can be awful on the inside. The next chapter will reveal why we shouldn't judge someone on their outward appearance.

Big or small, fat or thin, young or old, we are all pieces of the jigsaw. The support and encouragement to be original is what we need from one another right now.

Teach yourself how be braver, to know yourself that bit better, to let other people accept you as you are, or not at all. Dress and live the way you feel comfortable, not for the benefit of others. Enjoy your life more than you are doing right now. Try it – simple changes can have a measurable effect. As discussed earlier, our very existence is challenging and tough already, with all life's ups and downs.

Believe in what you stand for – it has great value. Hold your head up high and be mindful that every single one of us was created with a unique life purpose. Become very clear about what yours is.

Our DNA coding determines the chemistry of our bodies. The genetic information which has been transmitted from our parents' genes has been blended and fused together – how wonderful. Our distinctive features make us all individuals. Each complex characteristic and personality trait sets us apart.

Special Recipe

We are made from parts of other people – an incredible concoction of shapes and sizes, skin colours and personalities. All bodies are good bodies, so never, ever apologise for your body. You weren't born hating your body; you have been taught or led to believe this.

Let's face up to things: we may not have the perfect body, but who is the judge, anyway? We can aim to have a better outlook and understanding of our own individuality and self-worth.

As human beings, we are often going through similar struggles. Focus some of your attention on other people instead, and don't waste valuable energy thinking about how inadequate you feel. It's negative energy; remember to use that power and enthusiasm to help others instead.

Everyone has their share of worries, hassle and torments (sadly, some more than others). This is nothing new and it will always be the case. At least, you know that you are not alone.

Empathy and compassion for others make the world a much better place. I have known this since I was a little girl and I will believe it until the day I die.

Have a rethink; it's never ever too late to change or re-assess. You don't have to win the lottery to have a good life. You don't have to be a certain size or have a particular amount of money to enjoy life, either.

Like a battery, you have the energy and power inside you to initiate a change – a fresh outlook, a new you. Don't forget to keep recharging your battery on a regular basis. It won't run on fresh air.

Set yourself a goal and believe you can achieve it. Having confidence can make such a difference to your life. If you don't have bags of it already, please don't worry; you can start building up your supply. I will show you how.

Try to put things in perspective; appreciate and notice the small things. Make a mindful change. Mindfulness genuinely does work, and throughout the book I will help you reach new goals.

Human life is so precious; never lose sight of that. We appear to have all the science and technology you could dream of and yet, unfortunately, we fail to make sense of this simple yet complex human life.

Any brain pollution and debris that is inside your head needs clearing. Give it a good push out, make some room for new thoughts – good stuff, positive vibes. Nobody can pour from an empty cup.

This will not happen overnight, but with the right formula it will happen over time. I am here to offer support and to guide you through.

Chapter Two

Good or Bad Apple?

Having established that everyday life needs to be put into some form of perspective, I have come up with my own **apple tree theory** for you to think about. It's an interesting way of comparing people to fruit… bear with me.

As individuals, we naturally assume that other people have a much better life than we have. We convince ourselves that our friends, family, neighbours or work colleagues are having so much more fun and a better quality of life. *The grass is always greener on the other side*, right?

We all know how fake social media can be, and to that end I often think to myself… if, for argument's sake, you could gather together thousands of human beings, you could compare them to apples on trees. Or any kind of fruit for that matter – apples are just an example.

Picture in your imagination all these people in one gigantic orchard. An abundance of fruit (bodies), as far as the eye can see, growing together side by side, tree after tree row after row, acre after acre...

At first glance, all the apples look the same, but when you take a closer look, they are dramatically different from one another. Each apple aims to be the most enticing of all, the shiniest, the most perfect... determined to catch the eye of whoever is selecting.

But hang on a minute – looks can often be deceiving, can't they? Many of the apples are not quite what they seem. Our first impression is that they look perfect from the outside. It's not until you take a look inside – or a bite – that you discover what really lies within.

The reality is that some of the apples that look good aesthetically are in fact dry, bitter or flavourless inside. Other apples in the orchard may be far less attractive on the outside. They don't stand out or look colourful, shiny and impressive. Our first thought might be that they don't come up to standard. They don't appeal to the eye and therefore may get overlooked. Perhaps they are slightly bruised on the outside, or a funny shape. But wait a second... oh gosh, the unusual-shaped ones are genuinely good inside – so delicious, perfectly sweet and tasty, full of nature's goodness... we could be missing out on something really special here.

These fruits are rather like people. We have judged them instantly, on their appearance alone. How would you know, without seeing what was underneath the skin, that the outer layer is just a pretence?

To sum up my comparison: the fruits might look great on

the outside, but could in fact be rotten, bad or tasteless inside. The fundamental question is: what is more important: the outside, the inside, or both?

I have used this as an observation, but it does convey a very strong and important message for you to think about.

I mentioned in the introduction that I would talk about a blindfold; well, here is another observation or analogy for you to mull over.

Picture yourself in a room, sitting down, with a blindfold tied around your head, covering your eyes. In the room with you, and unbeknown to you, there are two people standing right in front of you. You can't see a thing, so you're relying on your other senses.

Person number one, for argument's sake, could be very attractive, dressed up in designer brands (male or female, it wouldn't matter), not a hair out of place. The whole outfit may have cost hundreds of pounds.

Person number two might be wearing something very simple, plain and inexpensive. Perhaps they have been gardening or just finished work for the day, their hair all over the place and no fancy or branded clothing.

You then have to spend a whole afternoon with the two people, so you can only judge them on their personalities, the sound of their voices and possibly their smell.

Tell me, would it make a difference to *you* what they were wearing or how attractive they were, if you had that blindfold on? Surely their physical appearance could have no effect or influence on you whatsoever?

Therefore, that person could be *any* size or shape, or have the best or worst skin imaginable. They could be a catwalk model, or somebody with green teeth, a knobbly nose and a severely disfigured face.

The important point that I am making is, yes of course it's nice to be looked at and admired, that is human nature, the peacock in us all. We like to look good and feel accepted; that will never change. But more to the point, surely rather than trying so hard to make the outer appearance look good all the time, what about working on the inside a bit more?

What's inside you matters and should not be overlooked. If the world were blind, how many people would you impress?

Work just as much on the inner you, rather than focusing constantly on the outer. If you are already quite good from within, then that's brilliant. Just develop your personality further; there is always room for improvement. Feed and grow your goodness. Make it sweeter, and maybe share that good stuff and contentment with others. Set a good example, pass it on – happiness is contagious.

Another example for you to think about is putting a tiny seed in a healthy environment.

If you nurture it and look after it, that seed will surely grow and flourish. If you leave it unattended in a poor place with no water, light or protection, it will not thrive anywhere near as much. Such a simple theory, yet we don't always put these things into practice.

Your body, mind and personality have not been designed for everyone to like you, or be attracted to you. The world doesn't work like that, thankfully. It's more about finding yourself and finding your tribe.

How peculiar it would be, if we all wanted to be with the same person. We are all so different and there is plenty of room for us all. We all have our preferences, as with taste in food, colours, music and books. It's a good job that we are individuals.

Reiterating the message of the book – remember to like yourself. If you don't like who you are, how on earth can anyone else like you?

Others may believe in you, but if you don't believe in yourself, none of it matters. Be at peace with yourself; don't be constantly trying to change. Inner well-being promotes inner beauty, which helps you to grow and flourish.

You are enough, you are special. Be strong and proud of this. You have every right to be living and breathing, just the way you are.

I am convinced that, in reality, the people we think look better than us are often feeling insecure too. They have their own share of worries and unhappiness, just like me and you. Perhaps they are feeling overweight, underweight, depressed, anxious, lonely, scared or insecure. Why assume that the other apples on the trees are better than you?

There really is no need to compare yourself all the time. Unfortunately, more often than not, this is what humans tend to do. Now and again it can be quite challenging not to feel insecure, when we see other people who are prettier, a better shape or more successful than us.

If you can identify with any of this, and at times feel a bit inadequate, shift your mindset and train yourself to ignore these disruptive thoughts. Focus your positive energy and attention on your very *own* good points and inner beauty.

I invite you to at least make peace with yourself. Your own body and mind are crying out, longing to be loved by you. If you can master how to turn a negative thought into a positive one, then contentment will flourish.

Hope lies in the changes that we choose to make, now and within ourselves. We have the power, *now*, to instigate the change.

All the apples belong, every single one, whether they are shiny and 'perfect' or dull and bruised. *Everyone* has a purpose and play a part within our society.

What we all need to be aware of is the fact that we are all unique and equally precious. It's important to recognise and celebrate our own individuality, this unique footprint that distinguishes us from the person standing next to us.

We can dress like them, act like them, smell like them (using the same perfume) and behave like them, but we are not the same inside. Greater happiness can be found when you stop comparing yourself to other people.

Make a list here of all the things you like or love about yourself. Memorise that list and play it back to yourself when you are feeling weak and insecure.

Chapter Three

Body Image
(How We See Ourselves)

Our genetic make-up means that we all have a unique body size and shape. We're all different and are not supposed to look the same.

Whether we like it or not, though, our world is obsessed with physical appearance. The combination of brainwashing and conditioning *from a young age* by the media and other outside influences has forced us to seriously doubt ourselves, questioning whether we should love the body we have been given. None of us are really born hating our bodies; we are gradually persuaded into believing that we have flaws and defects.

The importance of our body and its functions should never be taken for granted. Every single cell matters and has a special purpose; we need to respect our flesh and bones. Our face and all the organs inside us, especially our minds, play an important role in who we are.

By learning new ways to stop hating our bodies and criticizing our own appearance and even existence, we can begin to enjoy life again, without being over-critical towards ourselves.

Does a day go by when we are not obsessing about body image? It's virtually impossible. Thousands of negative thoughts come into our heads during a single day. A large percentage of them are probably the same old thoughts; sometimes bitter and negative ones, which then turn into feelings of insecurity and unhappiness. This type of thinking can wear you down.

Is today a good hair day? A fat day? A bad skin day? Our emotions can be riddled with toxic thinking patterns and processes, which drain our energy and fill us with anxiety.

The vast majority of human beings probably hear a voice inside their heads (this is, unfortunately, an involuntary way of processing our thoughts). As much as we try to accept ourselves, it's so difficult to ignore the nagging self-doubt and let go of the turmoil within our minds. It's like a silent plague.

When things mount up it can be exhausting, a real uphill battle. I believe that we all experience it at some point in our lives, whether we are young, old, male or female. Within this book I am focusing on women, which I tend to know more about, but these things apply to everyone.

In order to conquer this thought battle and put an end to all the nagging, tiresome insecurities, we really need to rustle up a serious amount of determination and willpower, focusing on beating this for good. Learning new ways to manage our emotions and control negative thoughts could be the answer. I hope you can learn from my experience and my mistakes.

We need to have heaps more self-awareness and self-love, and to practise having a positive attitude. Having a bad attitude towards our shape and size is almost like a flat tyre – until we change, it won't get us anywhere.

We have an emotional and moral compass within us, and this invisible/virtual dial is responsible for guiding us in roughly the right direction. If we become sad or distressed, our natural device/sat-navigation of the brain will let us know that we are heading off target (target being a happy place).

It's important to understand where *your* happy place is. If you don't know where it is in the first place, then it's impossible to get there and you have some more work to do. Sounds obvious, doesn't it? But believe me, it isn't always as easy as you might think.

Perhaps put some time aside to think this through.

Be aware of the fact that our brain conditioning and general outlook on appearance and self-worth has become extremely distorted and tainted by advertisements for the 'body beautiful' culture. A great deal of damage has been done. Sadly, in some cases it can last a lifetime, and unless we you wise up to it now and manage the situation, it could dominate *your* life too.

Perceptions of what is normal have been blown right out of proportion; the image-obsessed culture we live in continues to cause a fixation with *negative* body image.

No matter how many times we have been told that we are beautiful, good enough and perfectly fine, the devious voice within our heads tells us quite another story, somehow convincing us that we are not quite up to scratch.

Naturally, as humans, we all have an image of ourselves, a pre-set mental picture, whether it's a good or bad one.

Our subconscious mind, which can often get the better of us, can control our actions, behaviour and way of life. It's that serious. All this pressure to look a certain way and be perfect, as well as having a wonderful body, is simply destroying us. Believing that if we were slightly thinner or prettier, had better hair or looked cooler, we would be loved and accepted more by others, is doing great harm.

On a daily basis, the media, television, advertising campaigns and sexualised photographs make us feel unsatisfactory. They knock our confidence and surround our everyday lives, constantly popping up. They can be harmful, especially to impressionable and vulnerable minds. Teen minds, in particular, are being damaged.

As well as the front covers of some magazines featuring celebrities looking perfect, the inside pages sometimes show them losing and gaining weight, going out in public without make-up, or being caught on camera in a bathing suit whilst having some down-time on holiday. These have a similar effect on our self-image, from a different angle. Sadly, these stories continue to sell, influencing everyday people like me and you.

They bombard us with scandal, sensationalism and gossip. Anything to make a sale and get a reaction! These nasties, in my view, paint a cruel, dark and unrealistic picture of body image. This conditioning and persistent influencing is carefully and wilfully aimed at impressionable people.

Females I know have told me that the most negative part

of being a girl is the pressure to look good all the time, and that feelings of inadequacy play a significant factor in women's happiness and state of mind.

Many of them are miserable and unhappy with the way they look and feel, mainly because they compare themselves to others. Some are almost at breaking point with their insecurities, and this is when bad things start to happen, like self-harming and eating disorders. So many of us feel weak or imperfect, and are permanently on some form of diet.

It's so important to talk to others about your feelings; bottling them all up can lead to difficulties. Individuals can't always get the support and reassurance that they need. This is wrong and unnecessary, and it gets in the way of everyday living. Let me remind you: real life is certainly not the front cover of a glossy magazine – anything but!

How we are perceived by others seems to matter so much to us. In some cases, it can dominate our thought processes, and we feel reluctant to even leave the house without going through a painful ritual of checking this and checking that. Individuals could be missing out on lots of fun and, more to the point, food (which in my opinion is one of life's great joys) in order to stay slim and feel accepted. Some people are nervous to venture outside without going through a tiresome checklist. They are unable to feel carefree and can't even enjoy a normal day, because inside their head they feel so insecure and body conscious.

The younger generation cannot seem to focus on the more important things: for example, happiness, education health and well-being, because they are forced to waste time and energy worrying about their physical appearance all the time. It is torture.

A huge amount of time can be devoted to posting selfies on social media – with people in some instances taking up to fifty photos, until the perfect result is achieved. It's crazy, and as time goes by it just gets worse. No doubt it will continue to do so, unless we take back some control and stand up to all this social influencing. We really don't need filters and image-enhancing apps; this is so unnatural.

Kids spend literally hours trying to obtain the perfect self-image profile, which they think will prevent them being disliked or bullied. They sometimes have several social media accounts, in order to promote an unrealistic image of them-selves. Children as young as three or four are using mobile phones.

How many likes you have on social media sites can be the difference between a good day and a bad one. Obsessing over body shape can lead to dangerous, irrational behaviour, which can lead in turn to all kinds of illnesses, including anxiety and depression.

I have seen so much of this happening around me, and I'm not prepared to stand back and do nothing about it. We have to tackle this monster as a matter of urgency, before a major public health crisis explodes.

Our brains and our head space are being polluted and poi-soned, testing our emotions to the limit. For most of us it's an everyday conflict within our thought processes. We go along with all this behaviour, but it's always a struggle. Somehow, we manage to get through, but it doesn't take much to upset the balance.

Sadly, some particularly vulnerable and insecure individuals are facing even more of a challenge. If they are feeling slightly weaker or have significant personal struggles on their hands (including social anxiety), tension and worry can mount up much more quickly than usual. As a result, it can lead towards all kinds of mental health complications, emotional breakdowns and personality disorders.

Being thin, pretty or attractive, rather than being a good person, seems to mean so much more to our society.

We need to change this. The inside of a person should have more value than the outside, but, like weighing scales, the balance has been tipped the wrong way.

The inability and struggle to respect our own bodies is a crippling modern-day epidemic. What can we do?

The powerful, controlling media is *so* complex; it makes people slaves to their hang-ups and imperfections, doing all they can to hide their flaws. They haven't really got flaws, but inside their heads they are convinced that they have.

Just as there are warnings on cigarette packets and bottles of alcohol, there should be bigger and bolder warnings on explicit sexual content, and more controls, whether that's magazine front covers, audio-visual material, music videos (in particular), films or television programmes. Or, alternatively, the media should push and promote more images of 'real women' with real curves, spots, scars, cellulite and dimples. We need to see more real faces, real characters, real stories. We want more positivity and reality from the media, including inspirational, positive individuals who are sharing their personal accounts of overcoming difficulties – for example body shaming, depression or anxiety.

If we do *nothing* now, and leave things as they are, then things will continue to go from bad to worse. People need protecting. Without any controls, limits or guidelines, it is all becoming a loose-cannon situation.

All of this is debatable and controversial, and everyone seems to have a different opinion. As I mentioned in the introduction, even people from within the same family have a slightly different view or take on life.

I welcome your opinions on this. How do you think we should monitor and control this whole situation? Do you think things are OK as they are?

The important thing is that we all start to discuss these matters (maybe around the table), rather than leaving it for another time. If I can start the debate, then I have done my job. As I mentioned earlier, we can *all* help, and we can all make a difference. *We* are the people!

Whilst on the subject of body image, what does 'page three' actually mean to you? The answer may depend on your age. If you recognise the reference, how do you feel about it? Do you have an opinion? Does anybody actually care?

Surely, to women of a certain age this hideous display of women's bodies, baring totally naked breasts in a national newspaper (for all the family to see) was an unforgivable and unfortunately unforgettable practice. What kind of effect has that had on literally millions of women and girls today? More to the point, how did the media get away with this for so long?

Brainwashing

Brainwashing is the concept that the human mind, can be altered or controlled by certain psycological tecniques.

Pressurise someone into adopting radically different beliefs, by using systematic forcible means.

Persuade : Drill : Pressurize.

Another example to point out is the displaying of raunchy picture postcards (exploiting women), in a public place. Why do we need to see graphic photographs of bare bodies, bosoms and buttocks, spinning around on a metal carousel in a seaside shop or holiday resort? Who made that decision? Was it a man or a woman, need I ask? Surely this is inappropriate content – harmful and disrespectful to females of all ages. It can also make girls feel insecure and imperfect, adding to their insecurities.

Why do some publications, magazines and newspapers use terms like 'hotties' and 'crumpet'? This is so distasteful and derogatory – how do they get away with it?

Sorry about all my rants, but I do think it is important to discuss these matters freely.

One more observation relating to the world's deeply held differences. Certain groups of men are still insisting that they want (and are somehow entitled) to see more 'hotties', (a hottie being a sexually attractive person) in the public eye, whilst, in complete contrast, other males are insisting that their women cover up the whole body, head to toe, completely concealing themselves. (Males commands, all very confusing)

I am raising the point that women of *all* cultures are *not* second-class citizens and should *not* be exploited. Surely all females have human rights (as do men), but quite often they don't appear to have a choice. If it feels right to cover up for your creator, then I genuinely get that. I do question why men don't cover up in a similar way.

These thoughts and comments of mine are not getting at religion in any shape or form. I totally respect and honour people's beliefs.

I guess that it just goes to show We have *one* world, but clearly live in such different ones.

Going back to when I was growing up, I was subconsciously influenced by advertising and glossy magazines. Back then (the 1980s), I just thought that it was exciting news, stylish photographs and stories from around the world.

We felt privileged to be tipped off and to be a part of the latest trends and lifestyles. The thrill and sheer delight of buying a luxury, glossy monthly magazine felt amazing. There is no denying it was a wonderful experience, all those years ago. However, when I look back, as well as a few interesting articles on how to be a good kisser, what lip gloss to use or what to wear on a first date, there was a very negative and sinister side. Images, adverts and photos made me, as well as my girlfriends constantly compare ourselves to the pictures of women in those publications. Those powerful shots have left a lasting impression on my perception of body image.

Plus size, diversity and body positivity didn't exist in print, back then. There was no such thing as social media, or any way of connecting with people from minority groups. (This is where I have to give social media a great deal of credit.)

I recently had a reunion with some dear school friends of mine. Now in our mid-fifties, we talked about how these 'pictures' affected our lives back then. (We remembered some specific ones, for example sun tan lotion.) It was only when we discussed matters over a meal and a glass of wine that we realised we all felt the same way. We still, to this day, feel the effect that those powerful adverts had on us so many years ago.

For my generation, a lot of the damage has already been done. Millions of women have been emotionally affected, and in some cases mentally scarred and left with an unhealthy, distorted view inside their heads. It's going to be difficult, though I believe not impossible, to change.

Now it's happening all over again with today's generation,

and this time it's far worse. There are so many more outside influences. In particular, raunchy music videos are commonplace, but may leave a trail of destruction behind. They often feature scantily dressed individuals, groins, thrusting bosoms, lots of naked, oiled flesh and sexually explicit moves, buttocks, thongs, writhing and twerking.

I am really *not* a prude; I'm just a mother who is asking the following question: is it healthy for youngsters to be seeing this stuff?

Pornography is another menace – just a click away on the mobile device for children to be exposed to tacky, fake glamour and offensive material. Yes, there is a place for this, but it's certainly *not* for kids.

It is all too easy to let this slip, and to say and do nothing. I believe it is our duty and responsibility to safeguard children, unless we want even more social problems which could ultimately affect (and are ultimately affecting) us all.

Would men feel comfortable with being exploited? I doubt whether they would like it if their meat and two veg were out on display for the world to see (unless they were acting a particular role or starring in a porn film, perhaps).

Looking back, I don't think my male friends had many body insecurities. The magazines for them were of quite a different type.

In today's culture we don't tend to see a vast amount of male nudity, so why do we see women in this way so much more? How come it isn't equal? I guess we will never find a decent answer to this question.

I am *not* anti-men, but I can't stand back and let this happen.

In recent times, a lot of men have been found out. It has been brought to light that some of them have been using their power to exploit women, especially in the workplace. #TimesUp and #MeToo are now familiar hashtags on social media sites.

So much corruption has taken place, and many females have been grossly exploited throughout history. Thankfully the tide is now turning, and things are changing for the better. I love the fact that women are becoming more resilient, confident and strong, and that they are not afraid to break the silence. Females have always been strong, of course, but believing themselves to be so is a big part of their power.

Looking back, it took women years to get the vote, though thankfully it eventually happened, at least for some, in 1918. That proves how much more work we have to do to become anywhere near equal.

Empowerment heightens when women pull together. When one woman has the courage to speak out, it usually prompts and supports another to do the same. Remember me talking earlier about the ripple effect? It really does work. It's wonderful to see women gathering in groups to fight their corner and put across their side of the story. They will no longer tolerate this manipulative and unfair behaviour. This generation is starting to gradually fight back, in terms of body positivity and equal pay, etc. It's a wonderful feeling and a magnificent movement, thankfully here to stay. However, we need to be aware of the fact that nowhere in the world are men and women equal today.

I made a conscious decision a few years back to stop being influenced by branded magazines that were dominated by body image, and now I see things for what they really are. That's not to say that I wouldn't love to see many new positive publications. (There's huge growth potential here; publishers should be listening to real people.) Some magazines *are* doing a good job.

How do you stop being influenced by something? The best way is to buck the trend. The new wave of body positivity is perfect for uniting men and women of all shapes and sizes. It is growing by the day, by the click, but has not spread widely enough to date.

Let's use social media as a source of empowerment! Starting today with hashtags like:

#tacklethemedia, #effyourbeautystandards, #equality, #beyou, #selfbelief, #selfesteem, #respect, #understanding, #responsibility, #livingmybestlife, #bodypositive, #youareenough, #grateful, and #proud.

We need to take action, unite and say no to this unrealistic portrayal of body image. At my stage of life, I am interested in real inner beauty, authenticity and the thoughts and feelings of others. Perhaps this is an age thing, but I'm sure that some twenty-something individuals, and even younger ones, would welcome the change.

Writing this book and sharing it with you enables me to voice my opinions. I challenge you to find your voice, too.

Today's kids seem to want to mimic adults, by wearing grown-up clothing, make-up and accessories. Childhood innocence and simplicity seem to be fading. Children want phones and shoes and bags and all the materialistic stuff that goes with them. Overly sexy clothes seem to be in high demand. Manufacturers are responding to the demands by producing these fashion items, for younger and younger children.

Call me old-fashioned, but I was wearing dungarees and tracksuit bottoms until I was about fourteen years old, and my friends were too. Times have well and truly changed. Is it for the better?

When I was much younger, it was common to want to be like your mum or nana/grandma. Little girls would parade around, wearing their mothers' high heels, jewellery and make-up to look more grown-up and mature. At the time, it all seemed quite harmless and natural. Today's youngsters don't seem to play as many games (toy shops are disappearing from our high streets, though obviously online shopping has affected this too). Perhaps, in the past, a young child would prefer a boxed game or colouring set, whereas now they might feel pressure to choose clothes or/ accessories instead. Kids seem to want clothing, bags and gadgets (sometimes more than they want people). The fact is, they are made fully aware of all this 'fake' glamour, which gets thrust upon them.

Adolescents appear to be much more aware of sex, and some are sexually active from a young age. Sex education is now being delivered in primary schools. Compared to me, they seem so much more advanced and aware of their own sexuality.

Whilst we are discussing this topic, it's only fair for me to share some personal information with you. I just want to be honest and mention that I do have a healthy love life. I adore my husband and yet, deep down, I still feel very insecure about my body. I spend a lot of time worrying about my flaws. These so-called flaws, made up in my own head, are usually unrecognisable to my husband; nevertheless, they matter a lot to me.

In my mind, part of me thinks that I'm okay, and I feel quite feminine and sexy. The other half of me thinks that I'm a complete freak, too big to be worthy of a partner. I often feel quite manly, and basically in my imagination I look awful.

This *image* of myself has at times become a fixation. I tend to exaggerate my defects, making myself suffer with shame and inadequacy. Instead of enjoying the moment and celebrating the love and respect we have for each other as two human beings (something I cherish deeply), I feel stressed about my body. These perceived failings have caused such a huge amount of anxiety in my lifetime. I don't want this to happen to you, so please learn from me. Once I relax and am reassured, I am a different person, it's all systems go. My mind has such power over my body!

I know so many women who completely avoid getting undressed in front of their partners or husbands. They turn the lights off during intimate times, feeling insecure, ashamed, unsatisfactory and uncomfortable. Maybe that's because it's difficult not to compare themselves to the image inside their heads of the body they think they should have.

It is difficult to know what is going on inside someone else's mind (sometimes it can be difficult just understanding your own), but a lot of the problems, surely, come from years of body-image fixation.

There is no doubt about it: self-esteem affects your love life and sexual performance. A woman's mind has such a huge effect on her body. The mind is definitely an erogenous zone (often seriously underestimated, in my opinion).

Some females I know, or have come across, reject sex altogether, due to low self-esteem and body-image phobias. If only males realised how significant this all was. Instead of them simply responding to their *own* strong biological urges, surely it would help to reassure their partner first?

Luckily, women are able to talk about this stuff amongst other females. That's one of the reasons I think we enjoy getting together to chat over coffee, tea, cake or wine. It's good to talk, and it is widely known that talking triggers the chemical serotonin in the brain, which helps to reduce stress. If only women could talk to men as easily. See:

https://www.mindbodygreen.com/0-20069/why-spending-time-with-friends-boosts-your-oxytocin.html

(consulted 12/2/2019).

As discussed earlier, if these deep feelings of self-doubt and insecurity build up and are left unattended, they can lead to distress and unhappiness.

Sometimes, individuals can feel so bad about their appearance and weight that they are literally repulsed, or even feel guilty for being the shape and size that they are. Yes, they judge themselves and torture their own minds with feelings of zero self-respect.

I admit, I do this a lot. My insecurities spring to mind, but eventually, after a lot of deliberation, I reason with myself, more running commentary goes on, and then I'm fine.

It is important to find new ways of tackling these negative and destructive thoughts. The pursuit of thinness and fake beauty is having a devastating effect. Suicide has become the leading killer of girls aged between 15 and 19 worldwide. See:

https://www.telegraph.co.uk/women/womens-health/11549954/Teen-girls-Suicide-kills-more-young-women-than-anything.-Heres-why.html

(consulted 12/12/2018).

In 2017, nearly 6,000 suicides were recorded in Great Britain alone, according to the Mental Health Foundation:

https://www.mentalhealth.org.uk/a-to-z/s/suicide (consulted 6/1/2019).

Mental health statistics can tell us a lot.

I discuss females throughout the book, (because I know more about them), but need you to know how upsetting and devastating the figures are involving male suicides.

Male suicide is the single biggest killer of men under the age of 45. See: www.bbc.com/future/story (consulted 19/3/2019).

Self-harm, something that was unheard of when I was a young girl (which is not to say that it didn't happen, of course), is now an everyday occurrence. See, for example:

https://youngminds.org.uk/blog/kids-in-crisis-documentary-on-camhs/

and:

https://www.dailymail.co.uk/news/article-6731387

(Consulted January 2019).

A fourteen-year-old girl called Molly, viewed harmful content online before killing herself in 2017. The disturbing content on social media, may have been linked to anxiety, depression, self-harm and suicide.

It is our **responsibility** to stand up to these manipulating platforms which are **controlling** young people's minds. Why do we have to lose someone in order to take action?

https://www.theguardian.com/technology/2019/feb/07/instagram-bans-graphic-self-harm-images-after-molly-russells-death

It's terribly distressing to see or hear about other people feeling so worthless. When somebody damages their own body with self-inflicted wounds, it proves just how desperate they are feeling inside. It also demonstrates a particular form of 'coping with' and expressing unbearable emotional distress. It is a way of dealing with chaotic thought processes, **basically a cry for help.**

It's no wonder self-harming is on the rise and that an increasing proportion of the population is turning towards this distressing behaviour, involving self-injury. It is clear to me that this is a call for **more support**. This article in the *Daily Mail* reports that the number of teenage girls self-harming doubles in 20 years, and psychiatrists blame the pressure of modern life.

https://www.dailymail.co.uk/news/article-6029739/Number-teenage-girls-self-harming-DOUBLES-20-years.htmlt. (Consulted 19/3/2019).

More and more people are choosing to starve themselves

or to binge-eat for comfort, as another way of coping. Individuals are not getting the help and support that they need. They are slipping through the net, and in some cases, there is no net, as services are cash-strapped and support from the state is failing them.

Our society is struggling to keep up with the dramatic surge in eating disorders. Day by day, the numbers are growing.

Thankfully there is some hope, and there are ways of tackling these significant social problems. To start with, one of the most important factors is not to follow the crowd. The diet industries want you to do that.

We also need to work on having a happier brain. A lot of our emotions are determined by what is already programmed inside our minds. If we are having bad thoughts and feelings, we need to learn how to change them. We can and must find new ways of dealing with these massive struggles and torments; it's a priority for our survival.

Having confessed about my very own inner critic and my periodic self-loathing tendencies, it is only fair to share with you that I even have a specific name for mine. I refer to her as **'Freda'**.

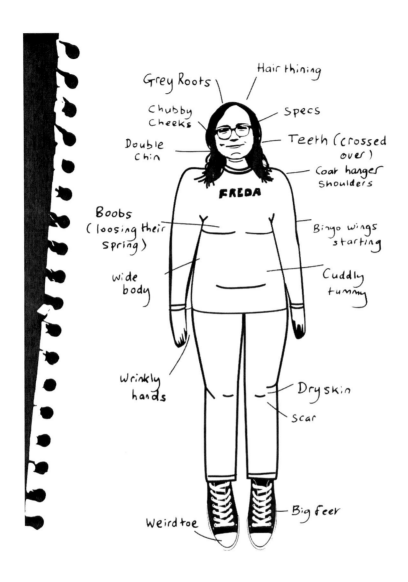

She has been around longer than I care to remember; however, I have finally come to terms with Freda being there.

In the past I could not always stand up to her. Somehow, she won the battle and had the power to get the better of me. But this is a thing of the past. I have learnt how to recognise my true value, finally believing in self-love and happiness, for the sake of my health.

From time to time I acknowledge Freda, in particular when I am spending time with my daughter, who knows me inside out – probably as well as I know myself, and relishes hearing my Freda humour and jokes.

It's good to be able to laugh about it. I laugh at myself all the time. I say things like: 'Freda is looking good today,' (obviously being sarcastic), as I push my stomach out that bit further, exaggerating my double chins.

It's all a bit of fun, but ironically it can also relieve tension. It's my own way of coping – I just shrug off my low self-esteem. It really seems to work for me.

Maybe you could choose a name for your inner critic? What about using the name of your worst enemy, or someone that really irritates you?

Let's face it, our inner critic can be dark, devious and destructive, so although we can laugh about it, sometimes it can take hold. Face up to *yours*. It doesn't have to completely take over our lives – we can either confront it or we can let it control us. Let's make sure it knows its place!

You have the power within yourself to change that inner critic into a positive voice.

Owning up to the fact that you yourself may have this subconscious twin could help a lot. It may be holding you back and stopping you from doing all the things you really want to!

Think back carefully, over the hundreds of chances you didn't take in the past because you lacked confidence. There were times when perhaps your inner voice got the better of you. Hang on to these thoughts and say to yourself, 'I am not prepared to let this go on any longer – it's time for change.'

We all have fears and anxieties, but don't forget that we are all equal; nobody is better than you. Nobody has any more right to be on this planet than you do.

Let's help ourselves and each other. We have hope for the future.

Chapter Four

Family is Changing

Whatever type of family you are part of – and there really are no rules – it is impossible to ignore that the family is changing in both shape and behaviour.

We think we have no spare time, and therefore listen less to each other. Conversations are dwindling; older people and their invaluable pearls of wisdom are becoming unfashionable. In previous generations, this is how we would have gained valuable information. If anything, in my opinion, we should be listening *more*, rather than less to our elders and trying to embrace their vision and wisdom. Older relatives hold the key to countless years of stories, experiences and vital knowledge; they have practical common sense that is well worth paying attention to.

I have always respected the older generation and never under-estimate the wise old theories and stories from the past that they care enough to share. This powerful wealth of expertise, knowledge and judgement is disappearing in front of our eyes.

If you asked older people what their advice to others would be (if they had their time again, that is), it might be something like: 'I wish I had done more, discovered more, and worried less.'

Older people's observations and family values are gradually being watered down. We can't let this continue. I believe that elders are integral to the population, yet the importance of togetherness in the community is not being recognised and valued anything like enough.

The people who make the rules for us all are not necessarily entitled or qualified to make these decisions. The balance isn't quite right. I think we need much more input from the very old (and the very young, too).

Who says that we should listen to some of the idiots who are running the world for us today? Why do we have to accept the status quo? It is our world just as much as theirs. (Don't get me wrong: we do have some great leaders and potential leaders.)

We, as fellow citizens, are all important and our voices really do count. It is a great shame that we do not have greater representation from real people, who are doing the job for love rather than for power and money.

Parents are spending less quality time together with their children. They have to work longer hours to meet the demands for materialistic things, under pressure to pay the bills because all the money has been spent. The appetite for the best clothes, fast fashion, shoes, bags and trainers feeds the demand. Our eagerness for extras and our high expectations gather pace. Instead of being careful and frugal with money, we are cajoled into wanting the latest commodity; we aspire to be part of a particular lifestyle, dressing the way we think we should be seen by others, not what we can truly afford. My old boss used to say to me: 'Cut your coat according to your cloth', emphasising the fact that someone should do as well as possible with the limited money they have. It is a very old saying.

Kids are getting away with behaving how they choose. Teachers, and even parents, have far less authority, and unfortunately kids are well aware of this and often take advantage or control. Regrettably, that can lead to less respect, resulting in a bubbling cauldron of behavioural problems.

Somehow, families don't have enough 'slots' left during the day to share each other's company. Simple things like eating together, carrying out household chores, shopping, walks in the park or around the neighbourhood, basic rituals and practices are slowly disappearing. Fundamental rules like right and wrong could become compromised, their message and importance totally undervalued.

It is very difficult not to give in to the demands of children, because the manipulation by other children is so great. Subsequently we feel guilty, and somehow choose to succumb.

Are we too tired for confrontation? Exhausted and worn out at the end of a long working day, it's so much easier to back down. It's a real weakness in today's society that families don't have the help and support that they need. In the past, parents would have more assistance from being involved with the community, neighbours, the corner shop, the church, perhaps a Sunday school, and youth clubs. All of these helped the whole community to take more responsibility. Was there more accountability? Kids would go to the park and play outdoors more, whereas nowadays we are afraid to let them out of our sight, and quite understandably so, as sadly the world poses much bigger threats than it did in my childhood days.

Back then, many of us had more time on our hands. We could walk to local shops, chat to the local shopkeeper and so on. This may sound idealistic, but in some ways it really was that simple. I used to visit the library or call on relatives. It was all about talking, communicating, listening, helping and supporting one another.

After all, how can we support and help each other if we don't talk? All these factors contributed to a wealth of understanding, producing a great sense of belonging and responsibility. Children could take pride in the community, or at least know what was going on around them.

Today, young people's lifestyles are quite different. Individuals are much more isolated. There is more online or television time; kids can spend hours on computer games or on YouTube – not speaking to anyone, especially older people. Youngsters constantly watch music videos, which can be quite addictive and damaging to vulnerable young minds.

Highly sexualised pop stars may be destroying young minds with their toxic influence. It appears to be commonplace that pop stars wear very little clothing – in a lot of cases just underwear. There is so much explicit sexual material online that kids can stumble across. This can be very damaging to young brains, shaping attitudes, values and behaviour, and this growing toxicity is bleeding into our society. We haven't got a first aid box big enough to fix the bleed.

So, who are our role models? Who can we look up to? Let me know if you can think of anyone. I know that we have an abundance of bad influences. Children seem to idolise influencers and celebrities, using *them* as role models. Developing adolescents try to discover who their heroes or role models are, gaining access to the *wrong* content can be damaging. Are we nurturing a generation of web addicts?

Who knows the answer? Perhaps we should try to discover more ways to have human interaction, connecting with nature and each other. Techie stuff is brilliant in the right context, but let's not forget the outdoors, creativity, sports and team games. We need to encourage young people to communicate more in person and less via phones and texts.

We certainly can't escape this modern life, and it is changing faster than anyone could ever envisage. Nobody can control it. It's easy for me to write about negative stuff, but that's not what I'm here for. I want to offer guidance, awareness and inspiration.

Let's re-ignite our passion for *real* life, connecting more with the earth and other human beings. Nature can teach us a lot so let's not ignore it. Do we really notice nature anymore?

Nature is defined as the natural earth and the things in it, the trees, forests, birds, plants and animals.

The deeper we look into it, the better we will understand everything. The great outdoors, fresh air, being free to discover new places of interest and beauty… Being indoors all the time could be stifling us; we are suffocating within unnatural air and lighting.

Animals can teach us a thing or two about life. They can be a good example to us: they live simple and practical lives. Some species show signs of compassion and empathy – they want to love and be loved. Dogs and cats don't just see the outside of a human; they see the inside too, loving unconditionally. They appear to be carefree, forgiving, loyal and simple. Other animals do this too; these are just examples.

Spending time together is good for the soul. There is nothing nicer than all sitting around the table together (regardless of what the table looks like; it could be a scruffy old hand-me-down one).

In many parts of the world, meal time is sacred.

Appreciate the simple things

Gathering together can enable individuals to share tips and advice. Because day-to-day life is hectic, there can be a lot to discuss and go over. Just listening is sometimes enough, sharing news and views and analysing the day's events. Understanding each other, caring and being compassionate, mean a lot. Things don't always run smoothly with families; teenagers will be teenagers, black sheep *do* exist and family members can clash, but on the whole it's kinder, if possible, to be as one. A problem shared is a problem halved, as they say.

If your family doesn't have all the right answers and needs a bit of guidance or support, then it's not too late to start researching ways in which to find it.

Make your own family self-help/guide-book/planner/journal; call it a workbook. It could be useful and fun at the same time. In the journal, add some cool suggestions to put into practice. Record your strongest memories – you could put anything in it, good or bad.

Your family traditions, things you remember as a kid, old customs, recipes or guidelines that your family have followed in the past... photos, tips your grandparents taught you – maybe even things they remembered from their grandparents too...

If something goes wrong or someone goes off the rails a bit, help them and discuss the matter together.

Don't ignore them or give up on them. It's never too late to get back on track. *Support at home, as well as at school, is crucial.*

Whatever you decide to do, put your heart into it. Focus on improving the life that you *all* have, **make a commitment**

to each other. I have always found that talking and sharing, listening and caring, understanding and relating to each other is what family is all about. It worked in our family and still does today (actually more than ever).

As well as working on your journal, you can all spend more time together, too.

A Few Tips on How to Make A Start

Turn off the TV.

Turn off the phones, for a little while anyway.

Give everyone a chance to talk.

Carry out some family customs and traditions.

Have a Pizza Night.

Have a Supper Night.

Look at old photographs together. *This can be fun.*

Get a record player.

Make some bread.

Go for a walk.

Watch a film together, with popcorn or ice-cream.

Listen to old songs. Play board games. Do some drawing/ crafting/painting.

Bake cakes together.

Plan some general 'get together' time for the future and see what develops. Even once a week is a start.

Have a tea, cake and agony-aunt session (discuss problems in a Q & A style set-up).

Cook a Sunday roast.

Play Monopoly.

Have a creative/making evening.

Sit by candlelight and **talk.**

Meditate.

Have a girls' night in.

Enjoy lounging in pyjamas and reading.

Have a clothes swap and chitchat.

Have a bath, light a scented relaxing candle.

Listen to a podcast.

Eat chocolate.

Dance.

Sit in a quiet place; give your creativity time to flow.

Create a café atmosphere; set the table with candles and wine.

Make a cooked breakfast.

Have afternoon tea.

Listen to a motivational speaker.

Have fun, because you will never, ever be as young as you are today.

Sort out your favourite *precious* photos and put them in a real album, not a digital one. Then put them in a metal tin or box, just in case of fire or flood. Photographs are **so** important, and we don't always have time to gather them.

You never know, you could actually end up enjoying yourself!

Add your own list here:

....

....

....

....

Chapter Five

Keeping Up!
(Society has its Demands)

The pace of life is accelerating by the minute. Society seems to thrive on speed, and for those in the fast lane already it's a tough challenge, while for others trying desperately to keep up, it's even harder.

We have acknowledged the fact that life can be arduous, and that just managing to keep up from day to day has its struggles. So, do we need to take our foot off the pedal, or should we keep it at full throttle? Something for you to think about.

Remember: we are all spokes in the wheel, equally part of this journey, so let's focus on making some improvements.

Like it or not, the next generation, the ones who are being most influenced now, will soon be shaping the future for us all. Ok, so we need to get things right, by supporting the younger generation. Instead of complaining about how bad things are, we could instigate a positive movement with real credible solutions for change.

The younger generation as a whole seem deeply concerned about environmental issues, as well as being more open-minded, honest, caring and understanding of the earth and their fellow man. Take, for example, the recent protests and marches that have taken place around the world. Kids have taken it upon themselves to miss school for one day and get their important messages out there to the world. This is commendable, a wonderful example of how we can *all* make a difference.

People need to speak out *now*, before it's too late. I don't mind being one of those people. Young, old – we should all have our say.

2019 is the year of change. We *all* have a voice, so make sure you use yours, or at least be aware of its power.

The bottom line is, where are we heading? What kind of world do we actually want to live in? I believe that this is a very important question and perhaps something we don't always address. What do you think?

We could also ask – what is this worldwide web doing to us all? Is anyone in control? Probably not.

Mobile devices are here to stay; they are now the remote control of our society, so I think it's fair to say that we need a lot more person-to-person, real world interaction. If not, we will become less human.

The internet, the single biggest invention within our

lifetime, connects us all and has become the foundation of our society, enabling us all to communicate and interact with each other with ease. However, it does have a darker side.

Within the book I am going to point out the negative side of social media, but before I do, it is important to acknowledge that it does have a very positive side as well. I use social media every day. It has many benefits, enabling us to communicate freely. We can stay informed and make connections (whether that's personal or for business). It is a powerful toolkit for helping people share information.

On the other hand, going back to the darker side of social media, human beings now have yet another platform on which to compare their lives to others. When we do so, our life never seems quite good enough, and we're always searching for that bit more, wishing we had extra.

You could ask – would we be as strongly influenced if we didn't have these means of communicating? There is a huge amount of temptation and pressure to spend money, money that we might not necessarily have, in order to look good, just so that we can 'fit in'. It's perfectly natural to want to be accepted in society, but all this comes at a cost.

Within our society, people are encouraged to live under false pretences, and tricked into acquiring things on credit, without the need for real, physical money. Despite numerous warnings, many continue to push themselves further and further, spending far too much and falling deeper into debt. This can lead to misery and despair.

It takes a lot of self-control and sacrifice not to crave for more. Personal debt is currently higher than it has ever been in history. See the following article, which gives figures for debts owed by UK householders in 2018. The total debt amounts to billions of pounds. See: https://www.bbc.co.uk/news/business-45343236.

The cost of living is not helping either; the prices of food and commodities are now at a depressing all-time high. We struggle on, worrying, panicking, gripped by temptation, and the economy seems to be up one minute and down the next. In order to keep afloat and plan our own journey, making it that bit more comfortable, we need to have our own set of rules. One suggestion could be to have our own 'road map', which would help considerably, offering guidance, focus and support. The map could include simple things like goal posts /dreams /visions set along a route. Having these goals can provide the motivation needed to stay focused, heading in the right direction, as opposed to wandering from place to place without any plan of action. Personal philosophy about health, wellbeing and happiness will enable you to take more control.

Global economic uncertainty can make us feel really down. Persistent bad news, breaking by the hour, with stories of doom and gloom on the television and in the newspapers, makes us feel even worse. It's hard to not be overwhelmed and consumed by negativity. All this misery mounts up, naturally we look for a way to temporarily escape, and a quick fix of retail therapy often seems like the answer. We look for an instant pick-me-up, and inevitably we spend. Click, click – products are in the checkout cart before we know it. We smile fleetingly, then comes the guilt, and perhaps the worry about the bill at a later date.

Many people are easily influenced by their friends, neighbours, work colleagues or TV adverts (which create the illusion that other people are having far more fun, due to the fact that they are spending), creating an illusion that having more gives fulfilment and status. This vicious circle of dog eat dog is such a waste of time and energy. Perhaps because we are made to feel weak and inferior to others, we randomly compete, frittering away time and effort, desperately trying to keep up. Meanwhile, the media continue to manipulate us more and more.

This brings me on to the subject of self-esteem. Possessions are not the answer.

Let's take ownership of the problem together. Ordinary innocent lives are being influenced by aggressive commercialisation. Our day-to-day thinking is being controlled; our children's thoughts are being manipulated. It is damaging and so unnecessary.

Many feel compelled to be the 'perfect' family, seduced into spending plastic money that they don't have, in order to look good in front of others. Sadly, for many people, buying a recognised brand gives more clout and status, along with attention and prestige.

Technology and science are advancing by the minute, but basic social skills and human interaction are not keeping up.

Some children have difficulty communicating with each other, things like sharing and caring, or using a knife and fork, or going to the toilet on their own when they start school.

Sad to say, things like trust, integrity, loyalty, care, manners, grit, backbone, courage – basically, all the things that money can't buy – seem less valuable, and when compared to materialistic things they lag behind.

Respect and looking up to someone because they are a good role model is losing its grip. As the generations slip by, disrespect grows. We need to educate young people about the importance of these core values, and if that means going back to basics, so be it.

Inexpensive, simple things that are hand-made or crafted don't seem to appeal to us as much as they did in the past. 'Make do and mend' is much less valued. Thankfully, some within our communities still hold on to this concept and appreciate its purpose. Hopefully, a revival is on the horizon, since during challenging times these old-fashioned traditions can be of great financial benefit.

Even relatively new clothes in charity shops or pound shops are now often only useful for rags; they have been made so cheaply and poorly that they are too fragile to be reused. It's much easier to throw things away.

This big brand 'fast fashion' is having a catastrophic effect on the environment. People's senseless appetite and attitude for 'more and more' is costing the planet. Without really noticing, we have gone from the days of making things to consuming things.

Making things is part of our DNA, and a throw-away society is not the right answer. Choosing to take and not give back will eventually have an effect. At the moment, many people don't seem to grasp this.

Many adopt the attitude: 'As long as we look good and feel thin, then who cares? Surely it is someone else's problem, not mine?' This irresponsible behaviour could be a recipe for disaster. Alas, heels get higher, breasts get pushed up further, lashes get longer, but do people get any nicer?

Surely all this focus on the outside of a person is fundamentally wrong? Sadly, many follow suit, copying one another's behaviour and lifestyles. If they can't look as good as their rivals or afford to buy the same expensive outfits and accessories, they feel as though they have somehow failed. This feels so wrong to me.

Take, for example, a social occasion like a wedding, party or christening. The cost involved for a guest to simply attend a gathering like this can be staggering. It can include outfits, underwear, beauty treatments, spray tans, hair, make-up, nails, shoes, gifts, cards and wrap, overnight stays, bar costs, travel costs, not to mention (if it is a wedding) the cost of hen and stag parties. If there are several family members attending the event, then the whole cost can seriously mount up.

That's when people can really feel social pressure to fit in, look good and appear to have enough money to keep up with fellow guests. Social and sexual pressure remains intense. Focusing on attempting to have the perfect outfit and the perfect body drives some individuals to the limit.

As well as being lured into spending, we also have to deal with things like 'gossip magazines', which are full of body images and fat-shaming content, which continue to cause unnecessary turmoil. They deeply upset some people, so why do we let this happen? Why aren't we fighting back?

Many women I know are trying to cope with this fiasco. When they visit the supermarket or local shop in all innocence, going about their daily business, it's difficult not to notice these tormenting and eye-catching glossy magazines. The constant reminders about our physical appearance can pollute minds and influence spending habits. It's hard to avoid having it thrust at us twenty-four seven. It is sending out all the wrong messages.

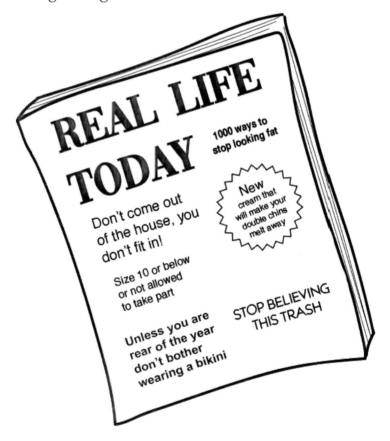

The beauty industry would collapse if people fought back. But they are blissfully ignorant about the mental health and well-being of vulnerable individuals.

I don't want any business to fail, but there must be a better way to sell magazines. What happened to positive and inspiring news? Surely there are people out there who want to read about *good news* – stories about real people with real bodies, not size zero air-brushed figures.

There must be so much 'good stuff' to report. People want stories about real life, not fake news! I know I do. There are so many inspiring human beings doing good things, and I long to hear about them.

Everyday people like you and me are *not* making the powerful decisions that inevitably affect us all, right now and in the future. This feels frustrating and unfair. The powers-that-be do not care enough, and they probably never will.

In the same way that a short advert can influence our choice of food or drink, this instant exposure to vulgar and explicit content can deviously shape young people's mind sets and values, and hence their future behaviour.

The internet is also a massive platform for sexual predators… just one click away.

We have enough conflict in the world already. There seem to be enough disputes, wars and religious strife, without our being in conflict with our own bodies too. At times it can feel confusing and bewildering.

As we discussed earlier, vast numbers of people across the world are covering up their whole bodies with layers of clothes and head-dresses, not showing an inch of flesh, whilst in contrast some individuals are having cosmetic surgery and going to great lengths to show off the results, with lots of naked flesh for all to see. Some dress in barely any clothing, leaving very little to the imagination.

Rather than concentrating on how we *look*, perhaps we should focus more attention on the simple things in life, trying to be grateful for real things such as our health, happiness and time, having a roof over our heads, being safe, secure and warm and having access to good healthcare. It is easy to forget how important these things are and take them for granted.

Billions of people worldwide still don't even have electricity. Many are starving and desperate, constantly going without water and food. There is so much cruelty and abuse in the world, so much crime, corruption and war. But instead of worrying about the world's problems, we selfishly focus on our own little world – for example, why do others have more than me – a better car, a bigger house, more clothes and holidays?

Stop worrying about what others have, try to pay more attention to our own issues as a nation. Think more along the lines of empathy, hope, positivity, unity and gratitude, rather than possessions.

I have stopped wishing my life away, wishing that Monday was Friday. You can do this too. Reality, routine and normality are good. Every morning is the first day of the rest of our lives, and we never know if it will be our last. I am sure that if you asked older people what they wish they had again, it would be time. So, think again, next time you wish it was Friday. The other days of the week are important too; it's not all about the weekend (even though weekends may be wonderful).

So much of a lifetime is wasted watching television. Why do we all stare at a box in the corner of the room so much? It sometimes feels as though we are robots, all doing the same thing. In some ways, our creativity is being quashed, as we waste hours of precious time watching the box – and of course that's when we see adverts and the bitterness and negativity kick in.

I will give you an example. If a child is 'creative and arty', it may be easier for him/her to watch a video on social media showing others doing art, rather than doing it him/herself. (On the other hand, kids can learn a great deal this way too, as long as they then put things into practice.)

Please don't get me wrong. TV is good in small doses; it can be very beneficial, educational, relaxing and a great way to escape and unwind. But remember, you don't need to rely on it as your only source of entertainment, every single day. Think of all the positive, productive things you can do if you are not watching television.

Our increasingly busy lives don't seem to have room for family traditions anymore.

Let's make some time, acknowledge the fact that we need to reconnect, improve relationships, have more gatherings, sharing quality time, and communicate more with our fellow humans, not necessarily using phones, tablets and laptops.

Let's be aware of how precious life is; let's think about it more and value it. Where possible, let's spend time with other people – including family and friends.

I'm saying this because I really care, and you might not realise these things until it's too late.

Chapter Six

Personality/Self Discovery (Trying to Fit in)

'Never judge a book by its cover', they say, but why do we do that with people? We are prone to judge someone, often within a few minutes, making an instant, first-impression analysis. Maybe we have evolved to make a split decision about a person? But perhaps we should ask ourselves why we automatically do this. How and why have we been programmed to do it?

Well, for a start, we can't go back in time, nor can we turn the clock back on advertising, social media and television. We are unable to change other people's minds about image, so maybe we need to find new ways of looking at someone, and knowing the true value of *real* beauty, appreciating what it is (inside and out).

I honestly believe that every person is beautiful, that each one of us is a work of art. Feeling good about yourself from the inside is what I'm talking about. Beauty is so much more than what's on the surface. Your inner sparkle radiates from within your heart and head, through your eyes and facial expression, in the form of electricity and charismatic vibes. **All these things form your character.**

Your personality, warmth and passion are simply a reflection of your soul. It will make no difference to your charisma if you are wearing scruffy clothes, have greasy, untidy hair and braces on your teeth, or if you have unruly spots and scars all over your face (scars add to our uniqueness). Attractiveness, personality and loveliness shine through everything.

In this chapter we will scratch the surface of some of the internal components that make up our personality. These characteristics determine what kind of a person we are and how the world sees us.

If someone is charismatic, warm-hearted, smiley, strong, proud, confident, smart, kind and captivating, then these individual elements will certainly radiate from within. These qualities really do exist, and they contribute to your overall beauty in a big way.

The opposite would be a cold, heartless, spiritless being, lacking any warmth or emotion.

If you already have stunning good looks then count yourself lucky. (Looks alone won't always help you get through life, though.) Whether you have stunning looks, consider yourself below average, or are somewhere in the middle (nobody is judging), then I want to help you recognise the true value of this sleeping giant within us all.

These attributes I've mentioned often get overlooked. This is real, inner beauty that has nothing to do with outer appearance. Whoever you are, whatever you look like, you can be what you want to be. Your very own body, with your exact size, shape and weight, is your story.

I would much rather spend my time with someone genuine, fun to be with, caring and decent than with somebody who looks like a plastic mannequin, with zero personality. Believe me, there are plenty of people like that on this earth.

So where does our personality come from? Behaviour patterns and character develop in early childhood and originate from our very specific upbringings and the role models, good or bad, in charge of our care at the time. Children are desperate for good role models, as we mentioned earlier, and they need to put their trust in specific adults.

Our genes contain instructions, transmitted from our parents, that produce our individual characteristics. Throughout babyhood and childhood (in particular, the first five to seven years of life), these interact with outside influences such as home life and school.

This hereditary and environmental information contributes to or determines a lot of our traits, thoughts, behaviour, ideas, values, memories and attitudes. Temperament may be inherited, too. The principles of right and wrong are formed at these early times, and the rules of conduct mainly grow from here.

Everyone's life experiences and backgrounds are completely different, each upbringing unique. Our environment plays a big part in who we are.

As Aristotle put it: "Give me a child at seven and I will show you the man." I love this ancient quote; it feels so apt to me, helping make sense of many things. Some people may totally disagree, but I think it's true.

Parents, teachers, relatives and other influencers can have a lasting effect on a person's life. I can't emphasise enough how important and significant this all is. Even society's values can be passed on to us at a very young age, so let's make sure they are the good values, not the bad ones.

Here is a famous quote that sticks in my mind, from American entrepreneur and motivational speaker, Jim Rohn. 'You are the average of the five people you spend the most time with.' Jim was a philosopher who left an incredible legacy of time-proven principles and wisdom.

See: https://www.goodreads.com/author/quotes/657773. Jim_Rohn, for example.

See also: https://www.businessinsider.com/tim-ferriss-average-of-five-people-2017-1?r=US&IR=T. The internet can be a great source of information for finding inspirational speakers and role models.

The 'TED' talks are excellent:

https://www.ted.com/recommends?gclid=EAIaIQobChM IgPot6iO4QIVB7TtCh2prAvJEAAYASAAEgIfOfD_ BwE#/

As I mentioned earlier, as humans we look similar, but we are *so* different. Physically, mentally and emotionally, we all have our distinctive components, from our minds to our fingerprints. Passion, which is the fire in our belly, our temper, grit, and how we react to certain situations, is born within us. Our emotions can be developed, improved or suppressed.

In recent times, we don't seem to be communicating with each other as well as in the past, mainly due to the fact that we now live in an internet society. What can we do to reconnect with life, instead of plugging in to technology all the time?

We seem to be joined at the hip to it all – in particular, our phones. It has crept up so quickly, I don't think we have really noticed. Interacting with a mobile phone instead of a human child (or a person of any age, for that matter) can be negative and damaging.

I'm not asking you to disconnect. I use my phone and computer every day; it is useful and a necessity for work and social. However, it would be nice, and a real personal challenge, to set aside maybe one day a week and try to make it tech-free.

We are all creative and gifted in some way; we just need to believe this and rediscover our talents. Use that time wisely, to unlock your creativity, de-stress and become human again. Getting into a habit will have great benefits.

Sadly, lots of people will never get the chance to create, or to live the life they truly wish they had. Perhaps they genuinely don't know how to; they may only dream about it. They may never step out of their comfort zone. The digital universe doesn't help at all either, carefully devising ways to distract us from the real world. I am determined to not let this happen to me.

Many of us are not even using half of our *full* potential, therefore we are failing to be inspired or motivated, for one reason or another. Sometimes folk don't even have five minutes to think. Gosh, we all need valuable thinking time.

It's good, every once in a while, to sit and think things through, to marinade your thoughts and make some plans for the future. When did you last take time out to reflect?

Trash television can easily take over most of any spare time we have, as well as our minds, on a day-to-day basis. It can also tend to make us a bit lazy (or lazier than we would be naturally).

Social media and games are extremely addictive and distracting. Think of how much 'real life' you have wasted in this way. Each day, real life gets pushed aside for a virtual version. If you don't believe me, think about it – make a note of how much time you spend during a week indulging in such things, in particular when you are bored or uninspired. (Some phones will work this out for you.)

As individuals we are never one hundred percent sure that we look good enough at any given time. We can never fully relax, just in case something is not quite right. There always seems to be an element of doubt in our minds, and this is such a shame. We scrutinise everything about ourselves, in particular the way we look. We watch television, look at the adverts and follow the crowd. If the crowd weren't doing what they were doing, would we be bothering?

It all goes back to what I said earlier about image… our outfits, hair, make-up, accessories and even what lipstick to wear (are we using the right shade, after choosing from hundreds of options?).

We try to convince ourselves that a more expensive mascara, which is 'newly launched' and promises to offer massive, full-volume lashes, will surely make us more fun to be with. This is not the case. It's not about the length of your eyelashes (although mascara may give you extra confidence), but your personality, magnetism and appeal from within.

Instead of embracing our inner sparkle and appreciating our uniqueness, we tend to instantly forget about it all, when we see another person looking physically more attractive. We suddenly become insecure and our self-doubt kicks in. Rather than feeling good about our own appearance, we immediately compare ourselves to the other person, as though it's some kind of beauty contest. IT IS NOT.

This is where we need our sense of self-worth to strike into action. All I am saying is, please don't be afraid to show the real you. Remember, what's underneath really counts, more than all the packaging.

Bad skin, spots and acne are not things I am ignoring here. I know that they are a real problem, in particularly with teens, but there is a solution. It is not impossible to improve your skin and make it healthier. Things like nutrition, how much water you drink, fresh air, pure, unprocessed food, fruit and vegetables and skincare regimes can have an effect. I totally understand the need for covering up bad skin, though.

As we know, make-up, skin care and beauty is a multi-billion-pound industry. We should use these things to give ourselves more confidence, enhance our natural features and be the best possible version of ourselves.

Avoid using cosmetics to make you look like someone else, disguising the real you. Being unique is much better than being plastic. Your skin is *you* and smells of you. How wonderful.

It's beneficial to take pride in your appearance, which can undoubtedly contribute to making you feel good about yourself. Being well-groomed can help with your confidence and inner glow. I understand that many individuals wear make-up to feel confident about themselves, not just for the benefit of others, and this is good. If drawing a black line across the top of your eyelids with eye-pencil makes you feel heaps more attractive and confident and it does for me, then do it. Whatever it is you need to do to add assurance, do it.

Be as spruced up and polished as you need to be, avoid being fake.

It is unfortunate that so many people do not 'get' the fact that attractiveness radiates from inside, and think it is all about the outer, fake beauty. Expensive jewellery, make-up, heels, nails, false lashes, silicon, hair extensions, spray tan, sexy clothes, bags and shoes all gives us more clout and self-confidence and can lift us temporarily, but don't lose sight of what's underneath all the armour and regalia we surround ourselves with. Diamonds, jewels, perfume and cosmetics are tempting, to make us feel feminine, sexy and sassy, but let's not overlook a simple, natural, fresh face, with a strong and confident attitude inside and out.

Vanity can often be all-consuming and, at times, can take over everything. It can leave us blissfully unaware of others, only interested in ourselves, our own life and appearance.

Having social hang-ups, doubting ourselves and feeling inferior are things with which we can all identify. I have been there, done that and now wear the t-shirt. These strong feelings of self-doubt can get in the way of our being happy and able to enjoy a simple, carefree life. I've felt that way myself, whilst going through a 'feeling fat and insecure phase', which is happening more often these days as my body ages.

We say to ourselves: 'I can't go out tonight,' or: 'I can't go to the party,' because we think that we look ugly or too big – so much bigger than everyone else who will be there. Others may look at us and think we're a mess. We assume they'll all be laughing at us and sniggering under their breath.

How many times have I heard this running commentary in my head? Why am I wasting precious time and energy thinking like this? Isn't it just a made-up story in my brain?

What we don't seem to grasp is that we *all* have faults: not one of us is perfect. These so-called imperfections make us real; it is all part of our character and personality, making us fundamentally who we are. Why should we feel guilty, ashamed, insecure and obsessed with our lumps, bumps, shape and size, constantly having to justify ourselves?

Whoever you are, and however much you are trying to feel accepted – just let it go. It's perfectly okay to be exactly as you are. Learning new ways to silence our inner critic would be of great benefit, otherwise it could destroy us completely. Don't let your inner voice cast doubts on your future plans.

Throughout my life I have met some incredible people along the way – so many strong, successful, brave individuals

– and when I think carefully about it, virtually all of them have had self-doubt and insecurity issues. They have had wobbly moments and tears have been shed. Honestly, this really does happen, to the most unexpected people!

This lack of confidence might mean, for example, not wanting to walk onto the stage in front of an audience to collect an award for doing something amazing that we all admire and aspire to – just in case they look silly, too fat or too thin, say the wrong thing or, God forbid, trip up in front of everybody.

And sometimes, sadly, instead of acknowledging how brilliant someone is, we wait for them to put a foot wrong. Why are we so hard on one another?

In real life, we all have issues and struggles, we hurt, we have challenges; things can and often do go wrong.

Your individuality is your greatest strength. Believe me, there is only one *you* on this planet – hang on to that fact.

People should respect you for who you are.

Many people find it very difficult to walk into a crowded room. Seriously, is everyone really staring at you and dwelling on the size of your stomach, chest or bottom? Perhaps some will be, but sadly they are victims of vanity, and who the hell are they to comment or judge anyway? Haven't they got their own issues and hang-ups to worry about?

Or perhaps it is all in our imagination and nobody is really staring at us at all; they are far too busy getting on with their own lives and thinking about their own insecurities. At the end of the day, do these things really mean so much?

Have a good think about this.

Isn't it more about you being at the occasion in the first place, having a good time, feeling alive and being a fun person to be with?

If I let my insecurities take over, all hell breaks loose, I start to think about all my bad points. I'm too fat, not petite enough, I have big feet, I wear specs, I have boring lips. I am too big, too tall, quite wide, I look like a man. My tummy is getting bigger, my breasts are slouching – perhaps I'm a freak after all.

In reality, I manage to wrestle and struggle with my inner critic, dust myself off and feel okay – quite good, in fact. On a good day, if I am wearing clothes that flatter my figure and make me feel more confident about my body, then I feel comfortable and reasonably okay. Whilst feeling like this I am able to reassure myself. Then, I can relax, enjoy myself and think positively, more along the lines of 'I am tall and strong, a good person; I have a warm and genuine smile; my eyes are quite attractive, apart from being hidden a bit by my spectacles; my legs are nice and long; I look relatively okay. I remind myself that I am a good mother, daughter and wife, and hopefully a good friend and work colleague too, and all that makes me glow inside.

I acknowledge the thought process that goes on inside my subconscious mind and prepare myself to find ways to overcome the frequent negative tendencies. When I am having a positive day, Freda doesn't have any power. She tries her very best to distract me, wheedling her way back into my thoughts again, but I don't let her beat me. If I give her an inch of doubt, she will take a mile. I still feel a little uncomfortable with my body size, but I can focus on my good points. Looking at my list, I am proud of who I am in the world, very proud.

We can all choose to feel guilty for not having the so-called perfect body, with flawless skin, chiselled cheekbones and perfect height, weight, thigh gap, breast size and bottom – but why should that make us feel somehow less of a person, and stop us from enjoying the life that we have?

So what can we do to avoid this relentless insecurity? Well, for starters, we can acknowledge the fact that we do have an inner critic and we need to take control of it; we must not let it ruin our life.

Something else that could help a great deal is to wear an outfit that gives you confidence and makes you want to smile. If you are wearing something that makes you feel insecure, al-lowing self-doubt to take over, try and change that. Plan your clothes ahead; don't leave it until the last minute – that causes panic. I have done this so many times, having been too busy to set time aside. When it comes to going somewhere important, I am frantically rushing about, tossing clothes around, wishing I had spent more time planning or just finding the right outfit which would fit with my insecurity level on that day. Once I had done that I could think about accessories and bags (or, God forbid, ironing).

You will definitely have more confidence if you plan to be calm and organised. This will beyond any doubt help with your self-esteem. You can then enjoy yourself at an event, because you know that any insecurities are all in your mind. Life is too short to miss out because of trivial stuff.

You don't need a fairy godmother; you need patience, organisation and confidence. Believe in yourself!

What we need to remember is our special secret formula, which is to have as much confidence as we possibly can. My secret is that I know inside that I am genuinely kind, funny, reliable, reasonably attractive, tall and charismatic, a good person, trustworthy and smart. The next time you are having a bad day, lacking self-esteem and convincing yourself that you *can't* do something or go somewhere or meet someone, just stop and think *I can.*

I need you to recognise the power of smiling, too. Smiling is *so* important. It is an unsung hero, our secret weapon and social tool. It can instantly improve *your* mood, and someone else's too. Smiling can be contagious; it relieves tension and helps de-stress you and, of course, others. It can also make you look and feel more attractive.

Your face doesn't need a language; it communicates with great ease and speaks for itself. Use it to communicate more with others, breaking down barriers and helping people around you relax. Smiling can help those who are feeling weak or needing support. There is always someone in need of help and attention, so practice being a good human.

It's kind to share your emotions – some of them, at least. I love being an emotional person. As I get older, I am becoming much more sentimental. I am passionate about pursuing empathy, kindness, helpfulness and generosity in the world. I never feel embarrassed about crying in public or expressing how I really feel. So, come on, do your bit, make a difference, be the change you want to see in the world. Together, as I mentioned earlier, we are stronger.

I am sure that you are a very busy person. Trust me, we all are, and probably will be most days, but maybe we can find some more time for each other?

Make a plan of self-discovery, self- care, starting today. Be supportive, understanding, caring, compassionate, and the very best person that you can be. This will have a knock-on effect on others.

If we all try to put this into action, our small changes can make a big difference. Say yes to a new challenge, a new hobby, an adventure, or just a bit of simple downtime.

Here are a few of my suggestions:
Draw
Sing
Create
Paint
Sew
Enjoy a bubble bath.
Walk
Think
Cook
Dream
Listen to music
Bake
Grow something from seed
Garden

Meditate

Run

Read

Write

Join a club

Cycle

Make a list of things you can do to take better care of yourself. Writing down a humble list, and committing your thoughts to paper can be extremely beneficial. Lists do work!

Organise your bathroom or kitchen cupboards

Write a diary/journal

Watch a film

Talk

Have a picnic

Do some sport

Collect flowers and press them

Have a pamper night

Think and plan

Sniff lemon zest

Walk the dog

Try aromatherapy; it's uplifting

Make a personal development list

Vow to yourself:

I'm going to start a journey of self-improvement. I aim to turn my life around. I accept myself today for who I am. I must not let my inner critic swamp me and take control of my happiness.

I will be kind to my body.

I have total respect for myself.

I will focus on the positive; there is enough negativity out there already. I won't be able to change anything with a negative mind set. I can't afford to waste time and energy on trivial issues anymore. Life is too short; negativity is toxic.

My stubborn attitude in the past is now being put to rest. Each day, as early as I can possibly awake, I will be in control.

I will make the most of my day and plan how it starts.

I will be as positive as I can be, depending on my circumstances on that day (my old habits will be hard to change, but I can nail this).

Today is important. It's not just another day.

I will practise mindfulness.

I am not going to wish my life away. I am not going to live my life just for the weekend; the other five days really matter too.

Tomorrow may never come – and no amount of worrying will change my future.

Yesterday has already gone; I can't change the past.

I am in touch with my body.

I am breathing, thinking, enjoying quiet time.

I need to clear away the cobwebs; my mind needs to open up.

I feel energised, inspired, positive, revved-up.

I am conscious of the fact that every single one of us has problems, obstacles and challenges.

It's all about how we deal with them, and I am dealing with mine.

I want to make myself as strong as I can be emotionally. That way I can help myself and then help others.

I must accept that I cannot change everything, but I can change some things.

I am moving forward and deciding what I want to do differently. I have a good vision.

It's my life, my rules, my journey, my choice and my destiny.

We all have that spark in us, and just one spark can change everything.

Chapter Seven

Good Times & Bad

Whilst writing this book I have been able to take a long, hard look at who *I am*. I have understood myself a lot better, as well as intending to help you. The whole process of putting pen to paper has been a real labour of love and I've given a genuinely honest account of how I feel about myself and the world in which we are living.

Every single person has a story to tell, and this is mine. It's my interpretation of some of the things that I think, feel and believe in.

Throughout this writing process, I have been totally upfront with you, and I have experienced some good times and some bad. This chapter is definitely about a bad patch, one that I hit during the final stages. I need to share it with you, mainly to prove that if I can get through all this, then so can you. I have never really experienced depression until now, and up to this point, had no cause to feel desperate and alone.

My personal life became very stressful and I was trying hopelessly to finish the book. As well as working and trying to keep up with everyday life's demands, I found myself becoming a sort of carer for my elderly parents too.

I tried to spread myself too thinly, and then things went from bad to worse. I became frustrated and lost, knowing that I couldn't give everything a hundred percent. Circumstances beyond my control took over my life; my beautiful mother had vascular dementia and my father was struggling to cope. Although I love him dearly, his stress and anxiety, on top of everything else, had a huge effect on me. Seeing them both suffer made me worry and feel so down and depressed. There were some other things too, but I won't go into detail. I might write about them again at some point.

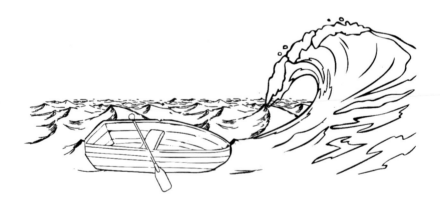

I am sharing with you some of my darkest hours, trying to explain the reasons it's felt as if my whole body has been stuck in treacle. It has been my sinking sand period. I have never experienced anything quite like it. At times I just wanted to give up. I found myself questioning my worth and all the things that I know to be right.

I have had a reasonably good life up to now, a happy one, but things really changed, and not for the better. Life around me carried on as normal, but I have been inside my own little bubble, which seems to be filled with a gluey mess. Sometimes you can be in a bubble and not want to get out of it. It feels like a safe haven, somewhere you don't mind being. You can be isolated and cocooned and yet, in other ways, you can see the outside world continuing as normal, but you don't have the strength to puncture the sides and leave the bubble. Part of you wants to escape, while the other portion wants to stay safe inside the bubble.

During this lonely, difficult and challenging period, it has felt as though I have had to 'let go' of a massive part of myself, a whole box full of treasure and riches. It's as though all my happiness, joy, and freedom of free spirit, including the many precious pieces of treasure that are buried deep inside me as a person, have been put into a box and cast aside – thrown to the bottom of the sea.

My environment feels stormy and unsettled right now. I can't see the box anymore; it is covered in murky water. It feels as though I am now inside the box, buried along with the treasure. I can feel the vibrations from boats passing by, right above me, but they don't know that I'm here.

I will stay covered for a bit longer, as we all know, time passes quickly. I feel that half of my soul is now under lock and key, and I have been in this state for quite some time.

There is a big hole inside me where the box of treasure normally fits. All my passion, creativity and positive energy, along with my entrepreneurial thoughts, ideas and aspirations, are locked away in there. I can't find the key at the moment, and everybody I know is too busy to help me look for it.

I am afraid that I will never find the key again.

I am not alone; we all have a box of treasures within us, laden with precious things that money can't buy. Each box will surely vary in size and content, but nevertheless, we all possess one and have the tools and skills inside the chests to enable us to build a better, happier life. The tools might be rusty, but with a bit of care and attention and some good old-fashioned elbow grease, they can be restored to full working order.

So often, and for many different reasons, we can't find the right key to fit the lock and open the box. It's that simple and yet, on the other hand, it seems impossible.

As well as not being able to find the keys, we don't always believe that we have this wealth in the first place. But gosh, let me tell you, we do. We can spend our whole lifetime aimlessly wishing we could find a box of treasure, sadly not realising that we have that precious material inside us already.

The world is missing a trick here, missing out on the wealth of talent that we real people have to offer. Society keeps us prisoner. We are chained to the television, social media, alcohol and other addictive distractions, and to many other damaging influences. If only we could get some clarity.

At Christmas time, for example, we reach for another type of treasure box, full of memories, special baubles, tinsel and decorations. Each one is a precious reminder of times gone by – sentimental objects we choose to keep.

We all have a Christmas box inside us, but the sad thing is, nobody asks to see it. Our valuable stories and colourful individual experiences get put away, and nobody has time. That's why it's so important to talk and share, not to lock everything away.

Another example is, if you don't provide somebody with a box of crayons, colouring pencils or paints, how can they colour? It's all about finding the colours and using them to paint a picture, your picture, your story. They need to get out there, look around, discover, think, plan and play.

The real me is always there, it's just that at the moment you can't see it. My light is on, but now it's dim, just a faint flicker, a low light, a pan of soup on the back burner, slowly simmering. My flame is not going out; I won't let it. A spark will come, and my flame will re-ignite.

The main thing is, I won't give up, although now and again it all seems overwhelming. I'm a shadow of the girl I was, but I will *never* give up. I am learning to cope with this bad patch now, with things going wrong and breaking down, bad news and disappointments, as well as things happening that are out of my control.

These rough times definitely make you stronger, strengthening your backbone, making you tougher.

It was bound to happen, and I felt it coming.

My period of depression and anxiety has helped me see things in a different light. I am convinced that this has been a good thing, that's it's all part of the learning process or bigger picture. I am turning a negative into a positive.

You certainly can't have good times without experiencing bad ones. We all have good and bad times – it's how you manage the bad times that counts.

My way of coping with all this unhappiness and frustration has been to eat and drink. I always turn to food in my hour of need. If I am feeling sad, upset or anxious, it helps me get through. It's not a crime or a sin to love food. The negative side, however, is that it has led to weight gain. I am well and truly a comfort eater, and I am not ashamed of this at all. At least I don't turn to violence or take out my anger on other people. Food is my safety blanket and lifeline. I adore it, even at the best of times. I eat when I am happy too.

But there comes a point when you think to yourself – hang on a minute, this isn't healthy. My body wasn't designed to be this size. It's putting pressure on my knees and hips. I need to stop abusing my body, punishing it and treating it like a dustbin. I'm not getting any younger and this spare tyre is making me feel sluggish.

My own body has been the last thing on my mind – the last thing on the long list of priorities. I completely lost focus on my body because I didn't care enough to practise self-love/self-respect. While the world around me has carried on being obsessed with size and weight, I have blissfully munched my way through pounds of cheese and chocolate, not to mention wine.

My coping mechanisms need to be seriously addressed.

This escaping from reality has now got to stop, apart from the fact I really can't look at myself in photographs anymore.

When you reach a point like this, it's time for change. You have to be ready for it though; nobody can force you. Most people go through tough times, and each one of us has a different escape route. Eating and drinking was my way of dealing with everything. But feelings of guilt and shame have come back – Freda is back in the building. This is my red light/ warning signal to stop. I need to stand up to her again.

Allowing Freda temporarily back is proof to me that she still exists, that she is always around, waiting in the wings for a weak moment, her 'curtain call'. It's as though I am on the stage and she thinks that she has a place as my stand-in. But she doesn't. She wants me to feel weak and give in; she wants to take over, but I am standing up to her.

I don't need **Freda**, I can do this on my own.

I am here to share my real experiences with *you*, and then to offer support. This book will give you tips to better understand yourself. You can then make better decisions and take real action.

Earlier in the book we talked about finding new ways to spend your time. I hope that you will endeavour to select a few suggestions from the list, then put them into practice. If you choose to give up, as I almost did, nothing will change or improve. Please believe that you *can* come through bad times; the power is within *you*.

If your life is in a rut right now, or you feel it's all a blur, there is no need to continue suffering.

List all your doubts, worries and insecurities below.

....

....

Then let them go! Put them in a box and throw them to the bottom of the sea. (Not literally – the sea has enough pollution!) *You* are in control of your existence.

Chapter Eight

Confidence
(Invest in Yourself:
The Best is Yet to Come)

It is so important to feel good about yourself. If you can find inner peace and practise self-confidence techniques, you could feel happier and have a better quality of life.

Confidence and mindset affect how you view the world and how others judge you. It's always good to invest in yourself. If you want to start really appreciating what you have already, and stop yourself constantly thinking that you need more and more, then discovering gratitude is key. Self-awareness and a greater understanding of what you have already is an essential part of being happy. Take time now to think carefully about what you already have.

Earlier in the book I mentioned that no one views the world the way we do, and I also mentioned confidence. What does confidence mean to you? We all have different levels, that's for sure. The dictionary definition is: "belief in oneself and one's powers or abilities". It's also about our ability to perform certain roles, tasks and functions, whilst feeling comfortable about ourselves. Self-esteem is how we feel inside about the way we look and think.

Do we feel valued? If we don't, then let's take a deep breath and face up to any emotional weaknesses we may be experiencing. The good thing is that it is possible to make some improvements and change our preconceived mindsets.

The command centre within our brains tells us how to feel and react, but we *can* change these thoughts. To become mentally stronger, we need to understand how our own thought process works – in simple terms, how we already feel about the way we are perceived by others. After all, if we didn't care what other folk thought of us, there would be no such thing as low self-esteem. These thoughts have been pre-programmed within our minds over time and they can be deep-set. These specific thought processes have developed and shaped our emotions.

To put it bluntly, confidence really is a state of mind. It is also a hundred or more little things. Social anxiety or lack of confidence are two more terms used to describe our lack of faith in ourselves. For example, we can feel it profoundly when we have to walk into a crowded room, or when we first enter a certain situation – maybe a party, a meeting at work, a wedding, christening, funeral or a gathering of some other sort. We become conscious of being assessed.

Are you comfortable, or are you sweating and turning bright red, with a lump in your throat? All eyes appear to be on us. Feeling fragile, it's natural to assume that we are the only people ever to feel this way.

Let me stop you there. We won't be the first, and we will definitely not be the last. If we choose to feel insecure and dwell on what people might be thinking about us, then we will always be a prisoner of those thoughts. Who are we trying to impress, anyway? We need to stop torturing ourselves. It is destructive and a complete waste of energy.

This vicious circle and mental turmoil quash any chance of contentment and happiness. But how can we avoid feeling so uncomfortable?

Well, simple things like mindset and outlook on life will help, and also a deeper understanding of self-acceptance. Self-acceptance is your judgement of how satisfied and accepting you are of your own attributes (positive or negative ones). Learning to accept yourself will have a huge effect on your confidence and self-esteem.

The term 'power dressing' was thought up for a reason. Sometimes you need mental support and back-up from your clothing. Wearing the wrong outfit for an occasion could cause unnecessary stress and make you feel uncomfortable.

Fashion is what you can buy, but real style is what you do with your clothes. Good posture can also make a difference to the way you feel and act. Holding your head up high and looking positive can help. Carrying yourself well, sitting or standing with proper alignment, reduces the strains on your spine, making you slouch less. Less strain will show in your face.

Take some deep breaths, stand up straight, smile, and force your brain to accept that things are all well.

As the saying goes: 'Put your best foot forward' – smile and go for it. It may take time and practice, but if you are consistent it really can work for you.

If you have a setback, please don't worry. Try to find a good role model and get some tips from them. We talked about role models and their importance earlier in the book. Spending time with confident, inspiring individuals can make a difference to the way you feel.

Identify *your* strengths and weaknesses; refresh and recharge that battery again. If you choose to believe that you are not good enough, not thin enough, not perfect enough, not tall enough, not pretty enough, then *stop*. Change this negative attitude. Change the narrative. You hold the power; nobody else can do it for you.

Let go of your anxiety in order to find real inner peace and contentment. You can do it; just give it a go. If you don't try, nothing will ever change. Don't be afraid to fail – pick yourself up and dust yourself off.

You are lovely – please stop putting yourself down.

Your new improved life starts here. How exciting!

Whilst reading this book, you have taken some quality time out to step back, reflect and carefully rethink what exactly you are doing with your life and where you plan to head next.

You know a little bit more about the society, what to expect and what we can all do to help improve it. Have you thought about whether you are truly happy, confident and settled? If not, how can you work on making a difference?

Set yourself some goals and make a to-do list. Write about your life and your feelings.

Most of the shadows we create in life are caused by standing in our own sunshine.

This book is about you. We are celebrating and acknowledging what it is that makes *you* special. If you believe in yourself, and that means with or without make-up and fancy clothes, you are heading in the right direction; these are your basics.

It's good to take pride in your appearance, to learn how to be well-groomed, to find your own personal style, work on that look and be original.

Ask yourself, 'What does my particular style say about me?' Your appearance should reflect and celebrate your personality, character and individuality. It should not mimic someone else. Remember: size does not matter anything like as much as people say.

I love the fact that there is only one of you out there – you are unique.

Remember we mentioned earlier that our inner critic dictates the way we see ourselves? Well, it's like that tyre again – up or down. So come on, give it a go; breathe in the future, breathe out the past.

Get to work on your mindset and cultivate your headspace. It's paramount that you stay positive and healthy. Drink more water, get some exercise and as much fresh air as you possibly can. Health and well-being is a lifestyle. Nourish your skin and eat the right foods – you really are what you eat.

Being well-groomed, polished and spruced will bring out the best in you, making you feel tons better, which will naturally lead to more confidence and peace of mind.

Make a note of what you want to develop and what you love about yourself already. To give yourself super confidence, create a mood board of *your* style. Try Instagram or Pinterest for ideas and inspiration (the good side of social media).

Lay out some outfits on the floor of your home and take photographs to remind yourself which items go well together. Use a journal to make notes. Planning outfits in advance will improve the way you feel and reassure you. Reassurance can help a lot with self-confidence (this really works for me).

Get busy, use some accessories, and don't leave everything until the last minute. Things don't have to be expensive to have style; just take pride in how you put everything together, think ahead.

Start charity shopping; it's safer for the environment if you use some second-hand clothes. Invest in some good quality classic pieces, if and when you can afford to, not forgetting that your smile is your best asset.

Condition your hair and spritz with scent. Perfume is a wonderful way to add an instant confidence boost – it awakens the senses and gives you a lift.

File your nails, de-scale your feet, exfoliate and de-fuzz. Hydrate your skin, buff and moisturise, get the best face cream that you can afford or read up on ones that have been featured online.

Remember, feeling good from inside about your personal care can make a *huge* difference.

You are in control of your existence; nobody else is. You can be what you want to be. Happiness comes from within. Your heart and your head are such important tools.

Life is full of happy, positive human beings. Try not to be taken in by the bad apples of this world, though believe me, there are many of them, including the violent, nasty, bitter, evil ones and the negative, narrow-minded ones. They want to pass on their poison to us, but we can't allow this to happen. There are more good people than bad.

Keep looking for the good ones, be a good one, and if you think that the world is going off (like fruit), make it better.

Share love wherever you go. Take ownership of the social problems we are all involved with; they belong to us all.

I hope very much that this book will make a difference to your life. This is just the beginning. Hold on to your enthusiasm. The energy spent on self-doubt and unhappiness can be turned around.

When you follow others and copy their looks and behaviour, you will always be one step behind them. Believe in yourself. So much in life depends on *your* attitude.

The message throughout this book is to keep growing, learning, changing and improving.

Step out of your comfort zone, enjoy life, enjoy family, enjoy simple things and be proud of who you are. **YOU.**

The End

RESOURCES:

Positive places for you to find extra support.

https://www.sane.org.uk/support Emotional support for families and carers (mental illness).

https://www.rethink.org/ Support for people affected by mental illness.

https://www.anxietyuk.org.uk/ Help and support.

https://www.samaritans.org/ 24-hour service offering confidential emotional support.

https://www.mentalhealth.org.uk/ Any mental health problems, including eating disorders and self-harm.

http://www.papyrus.org.uk/ Suicide prevention & support.

https://www.youngminds.org.uk/ Support.

https://www.b-eat.co.uk/ Eating disorder help.

https://www.supportline.org.uk/ Confidential emotional support, self-esteem and confidence. Telephone helpline 01708-765200.

https://www.childline.org.uk/ A counselling service for children and young people under the age of 19 in the United Kingdom. Provided by NSPCC.

https://www.familylives.org.uk/ Advice on parenting.

https://www.nhs.uk/conditions/stress-anxiety-depression/ understanding-stress/ Help with stress.

https://www.mind.org.uk/ Self-harm etc.

Acknowledgements

A massive thank you to my family, who have been extremely supportive and understanding, despite the length of time it has taken me to complete this book.

To my husband John, my rock, for believing in me and allowing me time and space to pursue my passion. At times I am sure he wondered what I was actually doing, on long, cold rainy days (of which there have been many), and many evenings through season to season. Luckily, we have a silent understanding; we are soulmates and share the same values and morals (although at times he does question my opinion on 'men'). He swears that you can live your life by this ancient proverb:

"The grass is always greener on the other side".

If you say the grass is greener somewhere else, you mean that other people's situations always seem better or more attractive than your own, but this may not really be the case.

Reference: www.collinsdictionary.com/dictionary/english/the-grass-is-greener

To my beautiful daughter Beth (the light of my life), who has had complete faith in me and been a constant provider of encouragement, reassurance and cheerfulness, offering a listening ear on a daily basis. She has also helped me with some illustrations.

To my parents (Joan and Leslie, two remarkable, decent human beings), who were both great role models. They gave me a very happy childhood and allowed me to pursue all my aspirations. They taught me so much about love, respect, honesty, integrity, family values, trust, honour and responsibility (the list goes on).

I have written the book for many different reasons. One in particular that springs to mind is that I am not prepared to put up with any more of this social nonsense. My purpose in life was to give something back. I have soldiered on, regardless of all the obstacles and distractions, in order to complete the publication.

Thank you, the reader, for showing an interest and allowing me to share my observations and such a vulnerable side of myself.

Several people have helped or inspired me throughout the whole writing journey. On occasions it looked as though the book would never be completed.

Contributors, kind souls, people who have inspired me:

Sheila Glasbey, aka Rosalie Warren, author and editor, for her patience and wonderful editing support and expertise.

Rosemary J. Kind, author and friend, for introducing me to Sheila and being a great writing buddy.

Liz Hurst, author, EMH editorial, for excellent service in my initial editing.

Heather Fenton, for support, advice and direction.

Cassie Fox, 'Reedsy' Book Critique.

Jane Dixon Smith, talented professional and experienced cover designer.

Della Galton, author, novelist and short story writer, friend and my 'writing idol'.

Joanna Penn, author of *The Creative Penn*, best-selling author, international speaker and award-winning entrepreneur. My writing 'role model', offering years of inspiration, information, writing support and up to date writing news.

Orna Ross, author, indie novelist, poet and advocate for self-publishing and creative business.

Swanwick Writing School, for giving me the confidence to put pen to paper: https://www.swanwickwritersschool.org.uk

Maureen, for changing my life.

Catherine, Annick, Del, Scott, Julie, Jackie, Jill, Debbie.